Advance Praises

Overcoming Self-Sabotage... this wonderful and motivating book shows you how to release your brakes and live an inspiring and inspired life!

~ **Brian Tracy**
President - Brian Tracy International
http://www.briantracy.com

Dr. Mamiko Odegard cracks the code to unlocking the power within through self-acceptance and love to overcome any and all challenges. *Overcoming Self-Sabotage* is a must read for claiming your personal power and experiencing new heights of success in every area of your life.

~ **Robert G. Allen**
New York Times Bestselling Author
http://robertallen.com/

Dr. Mamiko's book, *Overcoming Self-Sabotage,* is full of heartfelt stories of the actual process that anyone can make in getting past life's challenges. Her passion, caring, and wisdom shine through in any language! *Cada experiencia narrada llega a lo mas profundo del corazón de quien la lee!!* (Each "narrated" experience deeply touches whoever reads it.)

~ **Ma. Alma Garza Cano**, Founder and Academic Director
Cognitum School of Languages
Spanish-English Translator, Interpreter

Former Professor at Thunderbird Univ. ITESM-Mexico, Univ. of New Mexico, Univ. of Houston MA, Linguistics/Spanish Literature and Grammar Degrees from Montemorelos, México, Univ. of Texas-PanAmerican, Univ. Complutense, Madrid, Spain

Mamiko Odegard's latest book *Overcoming Self-Sabotage* is an absolute go-to guide for anyone who has been plagued by the pervasive feelings—duly reinforced on a consistent basis by the media and corporate advertising—of "never good enough." From her own forthright and clear personal story, and the compassionately revealed stories of some of her many clients in more than 30 years of clinical practice and coaching, Mamiko delivers hope and a way out of this vicious and personally abusive pattern of behavior and lays a foundation for a thriving life.

~ Amethyst Wyldfyre
Master Mentor & Medicine Woman
for Wealthy Women Of Wisdom
Http://www.amethystwyldfyre.com

When I first read *Overcoming Self-Sabotage: How to Jumpstart Your Love, Happiness and Financial Success,* the phrase by Albert Einstein came to mind, "Learn from yesterday, live for today, and hope for tomorrow." It is a rare person who is not affected at some point in their lives by negative emotions; it is a wise person who finds value in this book, which in many ways illustrates that while struggles and trials of life are present, we can choose to use them to grow stronger in the face of the adversities with which we must deal. The author addresses the inner-self and provides the proper focus for positive change in myriad negative aspects of life—from stress at work to relationships with peers, spouses and other family members.

The book is easy to understand and the chapters, each a varied topic, are short and filled with the kind of humanity and wisdom where readers share the author's experience in a way that fills the book with interest and compassion. Dr. Odegard writes in a unique style, and combined with humor, humility and humanity, is an overriding confidence she has what it takes to provide guidance, direction and the tools to act on her advice.

You may find you relate to one of the self-sabotage behaviors more than another; you may be enlightened to discover what you have always thought was the "norm" may be an area of your life where things can change... for the better! A refreshing and helpful book, the pages are replete with sense and sensibility — and a no-nonsense approach to recognize and deal with self-sabotage. I highly recommend it to anyone who recognizes change is the answer to the hope they have for a rich and fulfilling life – and willing to make the effort to engage in the process.

~ T. R. Stearns, EdS
Editor, Retired Superintendent of Schools

OVERCOMING SELF-SABOTAGE

How to Jumpstart Your Love, Happiness and Financial Success

OVERCOMING SELF-SABOTAGE

*How to Jumpstart Your Love,
Happiness and Financial Success*

Mamiko Odegard, Ph.D.

Biz Life Success Publishing, LLC

Scottsdale, Arizona

Publication Date: March 2016

Format: Perfect Bound, Hardbound, and Digital

ISBN: 978-0985158835

Copyright@2015

Published by:

Voices in Print | Biz Life Success Publishing, LLC.

Scottsdale, Arizona

Printed in the United State of America

Mamiko Odegard, Ph.D.

Scottsdale, Arizona 85260

CONTACT:

(480) 391-1184

http://www.drmamiko.com

Success@drmamiko.com

Retail Price: $9.97 Digital; $16.95 Perfect bound; $24.95 hardcover

Category: Self-help, personal development, self-sabotage, self-esteem, self-love, success.

Disclaimer

The names in the case studies that are represented have been changed and are used for illustrative purposes. These case studies and examples and should not be interpreted as testimonies of what readers and/or consumers can generally expect from the information. No representation in any part of this information and materials are guarantees or promises for actual performance and results. Any statements, strategies, concepts, techniques, exercises and ideas in the information, materials, and/or seminar training offered are simply opinion or experience, and thus should not be interpreted as promises or typical results of guarantees, both expressed or implied. The author and publisher, Mamiko Odegard, Ph.D., Biz Life Success, Inc. and Biz Life Success Publishing, LLC. Representatives, shall in no way, under any circumstances, be held liable to any party (or third party) for any direct, indirect, punitive, special, incidental or other consequential damages arising directly or indirectly from the use of any books, materials, and/or seminars, which is provided "as is," and without warranties. Mamiko Odegard, Ph.D., Biz Life Success Publishing, LLC or any of Biz Life Success, Inc's representatives' successes with these clients do not guarantee the same level of success for all individuals. These case studies are not intended to diagnose or treat medical conditions. Rather each vignette is designed to show problems and blocks faced by the individuals and couples who courageously directed their efforts to making conscious life choices to reach their goals.

Foreword

I am honored to write this Foreword! Dr. Mamiko Odegard is a master at coaching others to create personal change and positive transformation. She has a sincere passion for helping them overcome the self-sabotage that often interferes with the pursuit of dreams and goals.

You may remember me from being featured on the hit ABC TV show, *Secret Millionaire*. If you do not know of the show, here is the basic premise from show promotions:

"What happens when business motivational speaker and self-made millionaire James Malinchak is picked up by an ABC television crew, placed on an airplane with no money, credit cards, cell phone, laptop or watch, and is whisked off to an impoverished neighborhood, where he had to survive on $44.66 cents for a week?

The show features Malinchak leaving his current lifestyle in search of real-life heroes who are making a difference in their local community. He ultimately reveals himself as a millionaire and rewards them with a portion of his own money to further their cause by gifting them with checks of his own money totaling over $100,000. If you watched ABC's Secret Millionaire you know that James is no ordinary entrepreneur; he is a self-made millionaire with a strong passion for giving back and serving others."

Amazingly, over 10 MIILLION people watched me on the show! Whether I am speaking at a conference, walking through an airport, consulting for an entrepreneur or just hanging out at a coffee shop, I always seem to get asked the same question: "What was it like being on Secret Millionaire and how did it affect you?"

My answer is always the same. "The greatest feeling you can experience is knowing you have made a positive difference in lives of others. The show reminded me of that!"

And that is exactly what my friend Dr. Odegard and her teachings can do for you! Dr. Odegard will make a positive difference in your life through sharing her suggestions in this brilliant book. She is a speaker, author, coach and seminar leader who truly cares about assisting in confident transformations, using her unique strategies to empower you to overcome self-sabotage and live a more abundant, fulfilled life.

People, for the most part, are not aware of their self-sabotage. The effects of these behaviors are often not revealed for some time, which unfortunately, makes it difficult to connect a particular behavior to a specific self-defeating consequence. Fortunately, as Dr. Odegard notes in her book, it is possible to overcome almost any type of self-sabotage, and with the support of professionals like her, people accomplish it every day.

Self-sabotage impacts three important parts of our lives: love, happiness and financial success. Through the real-life stories found in her book, you will begin to understand the ingrained beliefs, thought patterns, and behaviors that cause self-defeat, and learn actions and strengthening processes that will reconnect you with personal values, goals and dreams. Dr. Odegard will help you to understand many ways we all get in our own way and reveals certain underlying causes of various self-sabotaging behaviors.

Some of her suggestions may comfort you while others may challenge your old paradigms. One thing is for certain. Dr. Odegard and her suggestions will stamp your spirit with an abundance of hope, inspiration and encouragement so you can reach new levels of success, fulfillment and personal happiness.

It is my sincere honor to introduce you to Dr. Odegard and her brilliant book!

~ James Malinchak
Featured on the ABC Hit TV Show, *Secret Millionaire*
Author, *Millionaire Success Secrets*
Founder, **www.BigMoneySpeaker.com**

Acknowledgements and Dedication

DEEP GRATITUDE GOES toward all of you... **each client** who trusted me and was open to new ideas and possibilities. You were courageous, determined, and dedicated individuals and couples applying your newfound knowledge and skills. I am so proud of each and every one of you for creating and practicing to be the best version of yourselves—while working towards and achieving your goals. In the process, a strong bond occurred between us in which we each appreciated the other and felt much warmth toward one another. Each meeting filled me with excitement and anticipation while instilling even more appreciation and awe of your progress and your building of personal resources. I couldn't wait to work with you, to follow-up with you, and share your excitement and delight, and sometimes your tears of joy... as you experienced and rediscovered the love that had been missing for so long within you and your partner.

Each meeting with you, my treasured clients, filled me with happiness, inspiration, and gratitude as you rapidly created successful and empowering patterns of thought and actions. The synergy of mutual trust, appreciation, and acceptance increased my passion of working with you to achieve your dreams.

Thank you for being EXTRAordinary in being vulnerable and honest while openly discussing problems and roadblocks as you shared your vision of a greater life for you. I am honored and so appreciative to you for including me in your journey! I am overjoyed and passionate that your life is becoming richer and more rewarding.

Eternal love and appreciation fill my spirit and soul for my husband, **Greg Odegard**, for his steadfast love, which supports me each day. Each of us needs to have at least one person who can be our cheerleader, that one person who can provide unequivocal love, emotional and physical support to listen to us, to understand our feelings and needs, and to assist us in reaching our daily and long term goals. Greg, I am blessed to have you in my life. You are my living miracle and a testament to how far a person can grow in emotional wellness when shown love and understanding, and prioritized as the most important person in the world. It is through your loving contributions in words and actions that I am able to be my best self. It is through being my best self and overcoming challenges and self-sabotage that I am able to help my clients claim their best self. Thank you, Greg, from the bottom of my heart. You and I were meant to be together... I cherish our love and each day with you.

Words and feelings of gratitude are deep in my heart for my dearest friend and editor par excellence, **Anna Weber**. She has been steadfast in her belief of me as a highly regarded person, professional coach, speaker, and author. Her keen intellect and her sage mastery of the written word have taught me numerous lessons on how I could become a better writer to more effectively reach my audience. She has encouraged me from the beginning of our work together to use various platforms so that people could hear and see my words to enhance their lives. Her literary and aesthetic talents have contributed to the formatting and the design of this book, which is destined to become a best seller with Anna's loving and spot on guidance. She is a person I trust completely as she freely gives from her heart. Her wisdom and skills are astounding and impeccable. I am truly blessed to have her as my literary strategist and friend. Thank you, Anna for being in my life!

A heartfelt thank you goes to my friend and mentor, **James Malinchak** who suggested that I write this book to showcase the types of clients whose lives I had touched and transformed. He was able to see beyond my titles of love, relationship, and performance expert and was the catalyst for my new identity as the "leading authority" in overcoming self-sabotage. James is an absolute genius in his ability to think out of the box with innovative yet practical ways to help build businesses. James' genuine care for me as his coaching student and his commitment to assist my career success, are forever appreciated.

Love, appreciation, and blessings are given to my parents, **Michiko and Enrique Martinez**, both of whom are deceased. I want to acknowledge and thank them for my experiences and their contributions that formed the person I became—one who cares deeply about others and who seeks a better life for myself. My father, a United States citizen in the military was stationed in Japan and married my mother. I recently realized and was grateful that my father was the person who was the catalyst for the miraculous opportunities that I had to thrive personally, educationally, and professionally by bringing us here. My mother loved me completely and was so proud of me that she believed I could achieve anything. I knew through their actions that they loved me in the ways that were possible for them. During the last several years of their lives, my father demonstrated an incredible turnaround. He let go of his impatience and anger and became a true model of love and caring, totally devoting himself to the 24/7 care of my mother who had become stricken with dementia. To witness and experience that profound love and tenderness from my father towards my mother was a gift from God. They were meant to be together after all, overcoming their many personal and relationship difficulties... and teaching a living lesson and tribute to how pure love can be manifested. Yes, true love overcomes all obstacles and brings out the best within us.

Table of Contents

Introduction

ANXIETY, DEPRESSION, STRESS, financial strains, loss of job or status, rejection, marriage, separation, and divorce—so many challenges naturally occur as you go through life. You simply can't escape the ups and downs of life. Would you like to know how those who have been battle-tested come out as they transcend crises in their lives?

As a professional, my goal from the earliest stages of being in the helping-healing profession stemmed from assisting people to feel a sense of hope, to alleviate pain, become one's best self, and to experience the joys of close, intimate, and trusting relationships, and for all to reach their peak potential for maximum success. I am a life and business coach supporting and partnering with people so they can attain love, happiness, and be and feel EXTRAordinary. I've worked with thousands of individuals and couples over the past 30 years as a psychologist, individual and marriage therapist, and now as professional coach. My hallmark is my ability to turn around problems quickly as I teach people to reach their goals literally in hours, days, or weeks.

Case studies are presented so you can be confident that you too, can have hope and easily overcome any challenges. The outcome is that you become stronger, healthier, and more resilient as you acquire more awareness and tools to better handle any and all challenges that come your way. This doesn't mean that you escape stresses in your life. Instead, it is about your ability to be flexible and have the best coping skills to minimize and successfully navigate distressing situations. It's about letting go of a victim mentality that you cannot do anything to change your fate. It is also about rising to embrace your power to make changes when you can, and simultaneously develop even more love and acceptance of who you are.

The coaching case studies that follow are designed to show you that others share the same problems and difficulties as you. If they can change for the better, so can you! I want to instill hope and for you to experience my ACT on Love™ process as you learn to be more tender and loving to yourself and others, and more comfortably take steps to change. By becoming emotionally healthier, you pave the way for greater love, happiness, success, and closer connections with others. Also, by taking steps to change, you positively influence those around you, and attract others to the new, confident you. You are able to influence present and future generations by leaving a legacy of love and acceptance through your own demonstration of proactive loving attitudes and behaviors that are being passed down through generations.

Are you ready to get started? I can hardly wait to help you move through your own challenges, be inspired, and know that a better today is already happening for you. It's not about where you start, or even where you are right now. It's about getting to where you want to go.

It's time to live your best life!

Chapter 1

Self-Sabotage
Be honest...
You do it. I do it. We all do it!

---

*Honesty and self awareness are the path
to an EXTRAordinary you.
Change for the better is already beginning!*

~Mamiko Odegard

YES, EVEN THE most enlightened individuals engage in some degree of self-sabotage. What is self-sabotage? It is to consciously or unconsciously make moment-to-moment decisions that lead to self-defeat, regret, frustration, anger, low esteem, a sense of failure and feelings of being trapped and stuck. Self-sabotage can be chronic, becoming automatic in the ways you deny yourself rewards and goals—while shortchanging yourself and leaving you feeling less worthy and dissatisfied. It is expressed daily in the choices that you make. Do you:

> Decide to sleep in for an extra 15 minutes, and have to rush to work or an appointment or perhaps skip breakfast?

> Run late and speed to your destination?

> Stop by a fast food restaurant and consume more junk food because it is fast and efficient?

> Pass up salad and other nutritious food for sweets and fats that satisfy your cravings?

> Shop and buy impulsively—trying to soothe your emotions, when you're sad, mad, anxious, or lonely?

> Stay up late and find it difficult to get up in the mornings and feel lethargic and less productive?

> Yell at your kids because you're irritable rather than take a few minutes to de-stress before walking into your home?

> Avoid standing up for your thoughts and feelings because you're uncomfortable with conflict, which results in later explosions over minor incidents because you've kept your feelings bottled up?

> Hesitate to directly state what you want for fear others won't like you?

> Pretend to listen, but really tune out?

Talk too much about yourself and miss out on learning and connecting with another?

Spend too much money when you know you'll be even more strapped when the bill comes?

Drink alcohol to relieve stress or anxiety or justify you're rewarding yourself for working so hard during the day?

Eat to relieve boredom or to feel better emotionally?

Let opportunity pass to express your love to the people closest to you each day?

Watch too much TV rather than interact with your family or start and complete your projects?

As a single, avoid initiating conversations with the opposite sex, because you don't want to come across as desperate?

Settle and date or marry someone whose actions violate your values, because you think that no one else will love you?

Procrastinate with social media when you have pressing tasks and deadlines to accomplish?

Live and work in a cluttered environment, wasting precious time searching for a desired document or belonging?

Allow others to make decisions for you and control your life?

Become a victim, letting events just "happen?"

Feel sorry for yourself and give up self-care?

Fall into anxiety and depression, but don't ask for help?

Become the "silent sufferer" and stuff your emotions while taking care of everyone else?

Stay in an unhealthy emotional or physically abusive relationship?

Experience uncontrollable anger or jealousy?

Focus on extracting revenge or making the other pay for your suffering?

Work hard—doing the same things over and over—in running your business and still not make a profit?

As you can see, there are a multitude of decisions you make each day. Do these decisions and actions help you or hinder you in having the quality of life and success you deserve? You'll find as you examine your day, that not all your choices, actions, and outcomes were "ideal." You say the wrong thing to your spouse, you bark at your office mate, or you skip working out because you're too tired, it's too early, or too late. Unfortunately as you accumulate these ways of undermining yourself, the results become more devastating— such as a loveless marriage ending in divorce, losing your job due to procrastination and unproductivity, becoming addicted to food, drugs, alcohol, sex, gambling, or shopping. The list goes on: experiencing lower esteem, frustration, and feelings of anxiety and resignation that you have no power to change your life... feeling stuck and staying trapped in the life you have created.

I know a very successful attorney with a thriving law practice, who feels too physically and emotionally drained to pursue a romantic relationship. She earnestly yearns to have a special man in her life that can sweep her off her feet, have a fulfilling emotional, intellectual, and physical connection and enjoy passionate sex. Despite her desire to be with a man, she throws herself into work, rationalizing that she needs to get caught up before really focusing on developing and keeping a relationship. How does that help Sally get closer to her goal of having a significant love partner? It doesn't! Instead she feels frustrated and exhausted. During one of our conversations, Sally shared her frustration, "I just don't have enough time in my day; I'm going crazy doing everything myself. I want a man to magically appear and rescue me!"

Overwhelmed with the day-by-day functions of running her office, Sally's escape is to dream of a supportive, loving partner by her side. Unfortunately that dream also leads her to experience pangs of loneliness and an all too familiar feeling of not being loved and having that special man in her life.

This could easily be a snapshot of many women. Are you singularly focused on work to build a successful business? Do you work hard at tasks and projects that don't quite take you to your goal? Do you spend too much time looking at emails, social media? Do you prefer to watch TV, or complain rather than work on your business plan or complete a necessary sales report? Or do you unknowingly sabotage your love relationship at home with no energy left to give to your partner or children? Perhaps worse, you feel so stressed when you're at home you find yourself being critical and irritable, ill tempered and short around the people closest to you.

You can sabotage daily in myriad small ways. You might not be able to blow your own horn in a convincing fashion when you give your "elevator speech," because you find it's too boastful to talk highly of your expertise or accomplishments. Instead when you converse with others, you don't confidently offer how you can assist them. Similarly, perhaps you have been taught that you should put others before you, and place your own needs last. Over time, this approach leads to depression and feelings of resentment, stress, and unworthiness—with you being less and less able to fulfill the needs and wants of your own life. As a homemaker or wife, do you really have to be Superwoman, and juggle work and home? Is it really necessary to feel exhausted every night by doing too much, not asking for help, and going to bed late to make sure everyone and everything are taken care of for tomorrow?

To seek perfection in all areas of life is another formula for self-sabotage. The more you seek it, the more elusive it becomes, causing you to feel you've failed or repeatedly come up short. Long term, this quest leads to lowered esteem and confidence as well as sapping your mental, emotional, physical, and even spiritual energies.

Yes, self-sabotage can and does affect all of us throughout our everyday lives. The case studies that follow are designed to help you become more aware of the ways you sabotage your happiness, love, relationships, and successes. More importantly, they illustrate how you can make dramatic changes to experience a more fulfilling and happy life.

As you become aware of the ways you contribute to your own pitfalls, you already begin productive motions to get you closer to your goals. You can minimize self-destructive choices and behaviors through awareness, commitment to change, and to choosing the best decisions and actions to show love to yourself and others around you? When you ACT on Love™, towards yourself and others, you open the doors to unleash unlimited potential to excel in every area of your life.

All change begins with awareness!

Are you ready to gain new insights and commit to being your best self to enjoy your ultimate life? If so, change already begins for the better!

Chapter 2

WHY Do You Get In Your Own Way?
What's Love Got To Do With It?

Low self-esteem is like driving through life with your hand-break on.

~ Maxwell Maltz (1889 – 1975)
American cosmetic surgeon and author.

PLAIN AND SIMPLE, you cannot reach self-love or self-esteem by holding onto limiting beliefs or destructive feelings you may have about yourself. When you experience self-loathing, or feel defeated, powerless, unworthy, unattractive unlovable, and inferior, you establish these feeling as barriers, consciously and unconsciously undermining your success. When you know and sense deep inside that you are somehow undeserving and won't get a raise, prestigious position, or a mate that will love you, the thoughts you hold inside create the reality of your life. Whatever you think and feel about yourself becomes your personal roadmap of achievements or pitfalls; they either contaminate your success or help you to achieve your desired goals. You become what you think... turning those ever precious thoughts into emotions that help or harm you. These emotions in turn, determine the actions that you take.

The simple truth is "if you think you can—you can." If you think you can't, then this becomes the truism for you. Some of you may consistently set goals too high, falsely believing you can achieve them. The reality is that you are harsh on yourself, setting unnecessary and difficult obstacles, which ultimately prevent you from success and serve to punish you. The more setbacks and failures you experience, the more these become imprinted into your brain—with messages that you are a loser, and you won't succeed. You are left with the big question, "Why even try?"

Interestingly enough, you were born with greatness. As a child, you were given gifts for self-love, esteem, security, and confidence. If you were cherished by your parents and shown love through frequent touch, being held, consistency of having your needs for food, comfort, and safety met, verbally

11

cooed and talked to, encouraged, smiled upon, and played with or given attention, emotionally and physically—you thrived, and allowed yourself to explore new situations and try out new skills. You could naturally be yourself, and you felt special, powerful, happy, relaxed and safe.

For those of you who didn't receive consistent care, attention, and affection (physical or verbal), you learned to stiffen up and feel uncomfortable with touch or being hugged. Perhaps messages were given to you that you weren't lovable or good enough; instead you received criticism and scolding for your behaviors and not doing a good enough job—whether it was eating your food, being polite and respectful, or your appearance not being pretty or cute enough, causing you to feel undeserving and uneasy when someone does give you a compliment. Some of you learned to keep your feelings to yourself with the perception that others didn't really want to know what you thought or felt.

Over time low self esteem becomes your nemesis, draining your passion, faith, and confidence in yourself and your ability to love, be loved, accepted, liked, and to succeed with tasks or goals. Without high esteem, loathing and criticalness become a natural part of you, prompting you to make decisions and take actions that undermine the person you are and want to be. You simply cannot outperform your self-esteem and your own love of self.

Have you ever known a person who truly has been successful in all aspects of his or her life holding feelings of unworthiness, inability to love oneself, and simply didn't like himself or herself? When you choose the ultimate rejection and abandonment of yourself, you open yourself for self-sabotage. You think, feel, and act in ways that are consistent with your deepest beliefs and attitudes you carry.

Your environment and the people who influenced your early years began to paint broad strokes of the person you would become: encouraging or stifling your emotional and mental development. Yet, time and time again, you hear stories of people who overcome adversity... using the difficulties of their past as a template of "what they didn't want" and instead found superior strength, persistence, and determination to overcome and to lead a more fulfilling, productive, and happier life. These became the heroes you admired, looking up to them as pillars and proof that you could become what you envision.

As a child, you were often powerless and at the mercy of your family or caregivers. Now as an adult or even as a teen, you have greater skills, resources, and choices that you can make. It is time to claim your God given rights to be precious and to be successful; to have the life you have dreamed of. You didn't get to choose the family that you grew up in. However, you can now choose to take control of your life and formulate beliefs and values that are healthier and serve you.

By changing your actions, you change your life.

Like many others before you, you too can achieve new patterns that promote your well-being and greater chances for attaining the life that you desire. The choice is all yours!

Chapter 3

Overcoming Shame
Does This Belong to You?
My Story

*No one can make you feel inferior without
your consent.*

~ Eleanor Roosevelt (1884 – 1962)
American politician, diplomat, and activist.

I IMMIGRATED TO the United States from Japan when I was seven years old. I was subjected to humiliating name calling of "Chinesey," "Chinaman," and "Jap," while kids taunted me with their "slanted eyes," pulling their eyes outward into slits. I felt ashamed of my appearance and my ethnicity. I not only looked different. I was different! I didn't speak English and couldn't read or write. I immediately became self-conscious and ashamed of my appearance, my ethnicity, and even my name. Academic struggles intensified my shame. I felt inferior, less than, and very different. I remember wishing that I could look more American with fairer skin, rounder eyes, taller, and with longer limbs. Early on, I even changed the pronunciation of my name, from "Mom e ko" to "Ma me ko." Yes, it was a subtle change, but softer and more Anglicized.

Many of you might carry shame. Shame is very different from guilt, because you don't have to do anything wrong. Instead you might actually take on shame caused by the actions of others. The important issue is that when shamed you feel less than, inferior, different, and flawed.

Two additional layers of shame emerged when I was nine years old and in the fourth grade. We lived in an upstairs one-bedroom apartment directly next door to my elementary school. I slept on the sofa or with my parents in their bed while we shared a common bathroom down the hall with another tenant. In contrast, my friends lived in large, beautiful homes where their fathers were professionals or successful entrepreneurs and their mothers were typically homemakers. My father was a low level enlisted mechanic in the Air Force and my mother started working as a waitress toward the end of my fourth grade. The knowledge of being poor and the

17

stigma that followed ate at me… causing me deep shame as I compared myself with others.

That unforgettable year, I had a teacher that I didn't like and struggled as class work became more difficult. Due to my father's different military relocations, I transferred from school to school… state to state, until we eventually settled in one place. Each time, I switched schools I advanced a grade even though I never had the basics such as phonics, resulting in skipping four grades in two years! Second shame: This stern teacher decided to not pass me to the fifth grade, further adding to my humiliation and loss of self-worth.

Luckily, that next summer, my parents had scraped enough money to buy our first home in the suburbs of Boise, Idaho. I was overjoyed and relieved that I was finally able to have my own room and to gain a fresh beginning at school where I could start a new identity. I thrived at the new school, finally learning and becoming a better than average student. This was also a time when I honed even more my art of quickly establishing deep friendships. Children liked me for being funny, happy, easy-going, loyal, creative, and also a leader.

Despite the positive things in life, when I turned 10 years old I faced another source of secret shame. This time it was my father's molesting me. He initially wanted me to touch his genitals and later began to fondle me. I would pretend to sleep when he would touch me—I felt powerless to stop him. If I told my mother, she had such a fiery temper that she could easily kill him. If I told the police, I would be shamed even more and our family would be unable to financially survive if dad went to jail. As I grew older, I felt the additional responsibility to protect my younger sister from abuse.

My parents showed love in their own ways. Both were affectionate verbally and hugged and kissed. Dad taught me different life skills, engaged with me in various activities, and talked with me about my friends. Occasionally when he could, he would help me with a poem or a drawing for an assignment. Mom showed me love by complimenting me—often to my embarrassment—bragging about me to her friends and her co-workers at every opportunity she had. She also showed me love by wanting me to have the best and bought the finest clothing for me. Yet, away from the public eye, both of them had volatile tempers: they screamed, cursed, threw objects and occasionally hit each other. Dad once threatened that if mom ever tried to take my sister away from him, he would kill all of us. When dad was angry, he'd lose his temper and at times, physically take it out on me.

I lived a double life. I was the cheerful, optimistic person that was friendly and outgoing. My friends were a source of great comfort. I kept it a secret throughout my childhood and early adulthood of the tumultuous relationship that existed at times in our family, never showing others any strains from my home life.

Before I understood what self-actualization was about, I was practicing it, trying out new ways to become my best self. I knew that there were certain circumstances of my life that I couldn't change such as our family's financial situation or my parents' temperaments. However, I could make small daily, consistent changes in myself to introduce myself to people, to make friends, to be a loyal and trusted friend, and to be proactive in achieving what I wanted. For instance, when my father was transferred to Turkey just before my 16th birthday, our family sold our home and relocated there during the summer of my sophomore year. I only spent one year there in

Adana, Turkey, because the military school only went up to 10th grade. I would have had to go to school in Ankara, which was almost 250 miles away. I wasn't going to a school in a foreign land that far away! Turkey at that time was primitive and an unsafe place to live for a young girl or woman. Instead of having to endure something so discomforting, I corresponded with my best friends, Becky and Ruth, and asked them and their parents if I might be able to live with them for part of the school year until our family returned to the U.S. My heart soared when they said, "Yes." Those days with my adoptive family, the Nelsons, were some of the happiest days of my life. I was loved and accepted by them, treated with respect, and we had so much fun together, in addition to many late night conversations with the twins, Becky and Ruth. I felt like I was in heaven not having to worry about abuse, feeling totally emotionally and physically safe... and a big bonus was that Mr. Nelson was the principal of our high school.

Life was sweet! My friends from grade school and junior high welcomed me back with open arms, and I was popular once again. Yet I missed my family, and took on the role of finding a new home for us by going out with a realtor to facilitate their transfer back to Boise. They loved the home I had selected for them and I was able to feel more comfortable, knowing we were moving up financially, as we settled into an attractive, nice middle class neighborhood fairly close to my high school.

More shame... although my friends and my dates liked me and treated me as their equal, I found myself feeling ashamed each time one of the "prosperous and financially successful" parents of my dates would ask what my father did. I would explain that he was a sergeant in the Air Force.

The parents, especially the mothers, would give me this look and send vibes that I was unworthy of their son. I exercised what I could control with excellent manners and politeness with my dates' parents, I continued to build relationships with friends through mutual discussions of thoughts, feelings, struggles, and dreams, as I did my best to be fun, thoughtful, respectful, giving, and become a great listener and confidant.

I had used the years since my arrival in the States to hone my communication skills, draw on the ability to easily and quickly make friends, and be supportive of and champion those that were disadvantaged in some way. I also befriended myself and somehow intuitively knew how to talk to myself in a warm, gentle manner so that I could create the life that I wanted.

I met my husband, Greg, at the library of Colorado State University. It was almost love at first sight with this handsome young man just starting his doctorate in environmental sciences. I was just beginning my senior year majoring in psychology. We started talking and laughing and didn't stop until four hours later when the library closing forced us to do so! Greg played a tremendous role in my emotional health and well-being. He totally accepted and loved me for all that I was, including my appearance and ethnic background. I knew I had met my soul mate! Greg loved the person that I had become. I say this because I want you to know that Greg was intrigued and attracted to me; the person I had chosen to become. That's right, I chose to carve out my individuality, to be assertive, to take risks, and to create events to benefit myself.

It wasn't until many years later, that Greg revealed he knew I was very different than all the other women in his life and he was falling in love with me when I surprised him with one seemingly small and insignificant, yet quick action. We had gone for a short ride in Greg's car and had taken along his landlord's dog. The dog became car sick and vomited. As soon as we arrived back, I rushed into his house and started cleaning up the vomit. He had never witnessed this before because his mother and sister would have told him to clean the mess. I use this simple example to let you know that you have choices that are open to you. My spontaneous action to clean his car made a remarkable impression on him with Greg becoming even more attracted to me. You can use almost any situation to shine, to become closer to another person, to empower yourself, and to raise your levels of esteem, confidence, love, and acceptance.

You'll be happy to know that I now accept and am at peace with my Asian background. No longer self conscious of my ethnicity or appearance, I warmly welcome Asian-Pacific Islanders and all other ethnicities into my life. I let go of the Asian stereotype many years ago.

My story of shame has a final twist. After achieving my Ph.D. in counseling and opening my psychology practice, I was in bliss. Life was fabulous with a loving husband, daughter, and many clients who liked, appreciated, and respected me. Unfortunately in January 2010, I was served a complaint from the Board of Psychologist Examiners. One of my clients had filed a complaint with the Board. I was in shock and disbelief that this could happen to me with over 25 years as a highly regarded and beloved psychologist. I went through the necessary procedures to address the complaint and appeared before the Board. 2010 was indeed the most difficult and stressful time of my life, not knowing if I would be suspended or lose my practice privileges. Suddenly, I found all the skills I had used as a psychologist in helping clients were crucial to my emotional survival and staying emotionally balanced: positive affirmations, visualizations, relaxation methods, staying in the moment, nurturing myself through supportive self talk, relying on the emotional support and love from my husband and my administrative assistant, taking necessary and proactive action, and drawing on my belief in God and the power of prayer. All these helped to sustain me and get me through this ordeal.

I never lost any privileges, but the complaint was upheld. I was consigned to a supervised probation for one year, but the Board was pleased with my committed efforts and determined six months later that I had fulfilled all my obligations and recognized me once again as a psychologist in good standing. Human nature is a funny thing. Despite the positive outcome, I felt ashamed again... for the first time in my professional career, which had spanned over 30 years. I had an impeccable record and reputation, but now my record as a psychologist would be forever tarnished.

As I look back on this event, much like my humiliation of my failing the fourth grade, I find the experience another blessing in disguise! I know now that by repeating the fourth grade, I became a better student who learned how to study and would ultimately use this to positively influence others. Learning how to study hard and attain my dream of getting my doctorate was another miracle. At one point in my professional career, I became an esteemed master college instructor who taught students in all my classes how to read, learn, and prepare for exams. Similarly, my traumatic Board experience led me to my current professional life as an equally esteemed life and business coach. Had it not been for my former client filing his complaint, I would have never found out about the freedom and benefits of coaching. I now have a career about which I can once again be passionate, feel fulfilled and grateful... every time I help another person reach their goals in record time! No longer do I need to categorize, label, or diagnose people according to mental illness. I am free to help individuals and couples to be their best selves, to be worthy, to recognize how EXTRAordinary they are, and to achieve ultimate success in every area of their life.

My story could have had a different ending. Being a foreigner and looking different from everyone else, moving from state to state, being poor, living in a dysfunctional household, enduring sexual, physical, and emotional abuse, being held back in school, and managing a major challenge to my professional career... each or all of these could have left me forever feeling powerless, shamed, and inferior. However, I chose the future I was to have.

Despite every difficulty, I never stopped liking or loving myself. I wondered for many years why this was so when everything in the professional literature indicated that those who struggle with shame have difficulty accepting, loving, and thereby, consciously and unconsciously choose steps toward self-defeat. I realized recently the difference was that I was blessed with a solid foundation of unconditional love. I lived in a household in Japan with my extended family: grandparents, uncle, and my mother. They held and kissed me, believed in me, showed me affection in various ways by praising me, teaching me and playing games, laughing and enjoying our time together, and giving me loving gifts, such as preparing special foods that I would relish or physical objects I would cherish. The key was... they treated me as being precious and unique. They were my family—my real life angels—who through their love, helped me to build my confidence and esteem.

This message is one of hope for all. Even if you don't currently possess high esteem or love of yourself, you can find those persons: teacher, friend, mentor, parent, or surrogate parent, who can support and affirm your specialness and goodness... until **you** can.

The reality remains... I chose to overcome my obstacles to become even healthier, and a more loving and caring person. And I also choose to share my knowledge and skills with you. You too can consciously love yourself and show that love to others and reap magnificent outcomes that create greater happiness, inner peace, and help you reach your dreams.

Are you ready to step into your awesomeness and become the EXTRAordinary you? Just like my story, it's not where you start... it's about the steps you take moment-by-moment that take you to your dream and the life that you so richly deserve. Yes, it's not where you start... it's the place or point where you arrive. May your journey find the greatness in you!

Chapter 4

Anxiety
In Search of Perfection

*Have no fear of perfection—you'll never
reach it.*

~ Salvador Dali (1904 – 1989)
Prominent Spanish surrealist painter

EACH OF YOU has had some type of anxiety and fear throughout your life. It might have started with fear of "strangers" who reached out to hold you, a fear of falling, bugs, frogs, and rodents. The older you became, the very fears that were designed to protect you, became anxieties. You worried about what others would think of you, or if you could jump as high as expected of you; you worried whether you could be clever or smart, or endure being teased or bullied. Even later you worried about grades, how well you performed in front of or in the presence of others, whether you fit in with your peers, or if anyone would want to date you. Your search for perfection followed you into adulthood, where you worried about jobs, status, and the financial strain of paying the bills, and if you could attract a partner who would love and marry you. Even later, you worried about being a parent and whether you were raising your children with the proper values and appropriate modeling of behaviors.

Patricia was just like you... and she worried constantly. Patricia was a joy to work with, and one of the first conversations we had was quite enlightening as she started our session by saying, "Mamiko, I'm just a jumble of nerves. I worry about anything and everything. I try so hard to do things so perfectly. In fact I work so hard that I don't take the time to make friends or have lunch with them. I just sit at my desk eating and working." She even hesitated to go to interviews, knowing she would be uptight, freeze up, and appear anxious. Even if she were fortunate enough to land a job, Patricia would then endure tremendous stress in adjusting to any new position. She lacked confidence in herself and created exactly the type of results she feared. This fear-filled young woman settled for a low paying administrative job, and became so preoccupied in doing things right that she placed unnecessary strain on herself and failed to notice the subtle cues co-workers gave her to engage with them.

Patricia blurted out, "I'm scared that I'm giving the impression that I'm too busy to spend time with others, or that I give off an air of being aloof and cold!" Deep down, she worried about not being accepted and liked; she also worried so much about her physical appearance and the impressions she might be making on her supervisor and co-workers. I could feel her pain when she shared, "All this fear causes me to experience difficulty sleeping at night. I can't help myself from mentally replaying over and over what I did wrong during the day, and how I could change things by trying harder."

Patricia became her own worst enemy. She had struggled with anxiety ever since she was a child, but ultimately decided she had enough! She came to me in her late twenties, seeking relief from her own inner turmoil.

I complimented Patricia on her courage and determination to become a better self. She couldn't talk fast enough about the torturous ways she caused herself to be anxious. The brain is a powerful organ, because it can actually create fears and anxieties that aren't actually valid. The brain doesn't know the difference between fantasy and reality; it only knows the information, which is programmed to react automatically and create sensations and reactions to your perception and thoughts.

The first step for Patricia was to take a stand for the change she wanted. After affirming she indeed caused her own setbacks and uneasiness, teamwork could take place. Together we conducted detective work to determine how she fed her brain the wrong information. We broke down the specifics of what she would say or think to herself and how those thoughts and feelings had impacted her emotionally, mentally, physically, and in her circumstances at home, work and around others.

You might recognize yourself in some of the following thoughts that consumed Patricia:

I'm always going to be a nervous wreck!

What's wrong with me?

Why can't I get this right?

Nobody likes me.

I'm not ever going to be close with anyone.

I don't need friends at work; I'm there to do a job.

What's _____ thinking of me?

They must think I'm so stuck up.

I'll never change.

I'm so ugly.

I'm unlovable.

No one would want to marry me.

I can't have kids; I can't even handle myself.

Who would want me anyway?

Why does everything have to be so hard?

Will this ever stop?

I'm stuck...I don't know what to do!

Can you see how Patricia actually sabotaged herself? She thought in terms of generalities of "always, never, and ever." She was a perfectionist who thought she had to do everything absolutely correctly—with an all or nothing mentality. I was not the least bit surprised to hear her say, "It is obvious I will never be perfect! I am a failure." Short of being perfect, she considered herself a failure... In Patricia's mind, "why would I want to risk disappointing or angering the people around me?" Unconsciously she had given up a long time ago.

Patricia also undermined herself by thinking too far in advance, such as marriage and having children when she needed to work on short-term gains such as building friendships. When you think in terms of absolutes and you think too far into the future, you find yourself being overwhelmed, and convince yourself you'll never get to your goal.

Ironically, before coming to me for coaching, the harder Patricia tried, the worse she felt. She put her efforts in a losing direction, and did nothing more than reinforce how hopeless and helpless she felt in the conquest over her anxieties.

By feeding herself wrong information over and over, Patricia had a steady diet of self-defeating messages that derailed her... causing her to feel even more fatalistic about not being able to change. That's why, when you feel demoralized and with a loss of energy and spirit, one of the first steps in overcoming anxiety and distress is to identify the messages or thoughts you repeatedly send to yourself.

Patricia became aware and began to understand how her critical, demeaning statements had set up a cycle of becoming even more vigilant about how she handled tasks. These perpetual defeating messages also made sure that she kept her guard up around others, offering few comments and little glimpses of others getting to know her.

As her awareness increased, Patricia was better able to remember and be comfortable enough in my presence to share another critical awareness with me, "I am beginning to remember how often my mother criticized me for not being perfect! My grades, the way I dressed, my hairstyles, my face, my attitude, and the way I spoke and responded to diverse situations, were all fair game for mom's opportunities to demean me. Rarely did a week go by my mom didn't tell me how I looked ridiculous, and others wouldn't like me." As I leaned in closer to her, to more fully connect and show my caring and understanding, she painfully recalled that whatever she did was never quite to her mother's satisfaction.

After this realization, Patricia changed from the inner critic to one who had more compassion for herself. She realized that she frequently sought approval from others and made a shift to treat herself exactly how she wanted to be thought of by others and began demonstrating affection to herself. She learned to love and accept herself through conscious loving™ in which she mindfully choose to stop beating up on herself. One of the most fulfilling days for me was when Patricia announced, "In place of all the worthless self-talk and behavior, I can now choose words that support, encourage, and show me self-love!"

No longer satisfied to be the wallflower, Patricia was eager to learn new communication skills. "I've worried so long about being too boring and being too occupied with everybody's perceptions of me that I don't know how to really start conversations." As we worked, not only did Patricia develop effective skills for initiating and listening to people, she began to reveal parts about herself to others. Each week, I could see her literally blossoming in front of me. She began to attract others with her smile, direct eye contact, and ability to listen. The caring that Patricia was now showing herself... she now transferred those same compassionate gestures to others.

Patricia is now happier than she's ever been. With her frown lines softened, she smiles often and is now comfortable around her supervisor and office mates. She is being included in social gatherings, making friends and even dating. She is finally able to be at peace and sleep problems are a thing of the past. Her previously tortured mind is quiet and full of appreciation for each day. Life is good and gets better each day.

Chapter 5

Overcoming Depression
"All I Need is Love"

To love oneself is the beginning of a life-long romance.

~ Oscar Wilde (1854 – 1900)
Irish author, playwright and poet.

YOU HAVE EXPERIENCED life with its ups and downs. Have you ever felt hopeless or that life had little meaning and left you lost and distraught? That's exactly what Ken experienced. His physician quickly referred Ken to me after she became alarmed that Ken was feeling suicidal. An appointment was immediately made, and Ken appeared at my office confused, depressed, and discouraged.

Ken, 42 years old, had experienced several setbacks. His girlfriend had taken advantage of Ken's kind and generous nature, and broken up with him after he had jeopardized his financial well-being. He was passed over for a promotion and was grinding away at a job that was unfulfilling. He struggled to pay his bills and lived paycheck to paycheck. Although a likeable guy, he didn't have close friends, which made the loss of his girlfriend even more devastating for him. He considered himself to be unattractive, with little to offer her or any other woman because he had lost his savings, was in debt, and about to lose his home. Ken couldn't see a way out of his dilemma and felt ashamed of his life. Life for him consisted of the same unfulfilling routine: go to work and come home to an empty house. He dreaded the prospect of moving into a small one-bedroom apartment.

The day I met Ken, we initially talked for two hours. I had another appointment, but asked Ken to come back an hour later. He eagerly agreed and on his return we talked for another two hours. I let him know I was totally committed to help get past his obstacles and would teach him skills to overcome his depression. He felt the genuineness of my compassion and remarked, "You are the first person who ever showed such interest and concern for me." His mood of depression changed before my eyes. I knew that even after our first meeting... he would be safe.

I saw Ken the next day for three hours. He was like a new person; he no longer felt suicidal, and instead felt uplifted, hopeful, and ready to share more of his feelings and background. My belief in Ken that he was a worthy individual made the difference for him. As a professional, I was more than touched when Ken started one of our conversations by stating, "Mamiko, no one, and I mean no one, has ever talked to me the way you did. You made me feel important, and let me know I am special and can create a life I want!" He expressed how even the simple act during our first meeting of giving him my personal phone number that he could use to contact me directly added to his comfort and trust in me.

Within the framework of safety and empowerment, Ken learned various strategies to immediately use to diffuse his sense of sadness, low self-esteem, and feelings of powerlessness. These were fine tuned during later sessions as we discussed the different events in his life that contributed to him feeling so unworthy. He never remembered having a mentor or parent who encouraged him or praised who he was or his efforts. Ken realized this was why he responded so positively to my support of him and my commitment to stand by his side. Suddenly he was filled with new feelings and a belief that he was valuable and lovable.

Unknowingly, the depths of despair and Ken's willingness to seek help provided the impetus for him to emerge victoriously as a winner. Limiting beliefs and destructive feelings of self-contempt, which undermined his ability to feel worthy and succeed, no longer shackled him.

He learned how to initiate conversations and engage others to further empower himself.

I'm happy to report even two years after our working together Ken is doing fabulously. I'm not sure which of us felt more ecstatic the day Ken called to share his progress; I could feel the shift in energies as dramatic and palpable as he extolled, "Thanks to my time with you, I am living a happier, richer life with friends and enjoying my work more. I think maybe I really called to tell you I am engaged and excited about getting married. I just feel so blessed in how my life has changed. You know, Mamiko, sometimes... sometimes all it takes is a compassionate and caring individual to affirm and encourage someone in order to guide them to all the possibilities that are open to them. You were that person for me, and I thank you."

Chapter 6

Insecurity
The Controlling Executive

*There is nothing noble about being superior
to some other man.
The true nobility is in being superior to your
previous self.*

~ Hindu Proverb

DURING MY CAREER as a psychologist, therapist, and coach, I have worked with many high-powered executives. For the most part, they had reached their level of success, because they were driven, but tended to be over controlling and micromanaged others at their workplace and at home. They would come in, reluctantly, often after insistence by their wives, who found them unbearable to live with. Some would accompany their wives when their marriage was on the rocks—their relationship threatened by a possible divorce.

Neal was a CEO who had immense wealth and influence after negotiating multi-million dollar deals nationally and internationally. His emotions primarily shifted from loving to anger to fear, with relatively little exhibition of other emotions. He was self made and proud of it, continually working hard and insisting he be filled in on all details of business plans before he would give employees his approval to go ahead with actions.

Several problems with Neal existed:

Despite Neal's business acumen and success, he was insecure with himself;

Due to his feelings of insecurity, he needed to overly manage his employees, not allowing them the freedom to develop his company to greater heights;

He was driven and spent too much of his energies focused on improving profitability of his company;

He didn't know how to establish clear boundaries of behavior with employees and his family, and treated his wife as a subordinate;

He ruled with an iron fist, making it difficult for him to be emotionally connected and loving with his wife and children;

He was a black and white thinker—situations were good or bad, right or wrong;

His way was the correct one;

He didn't know how to listen, and frequently interrupted and made assumptions of what the other needed, wanted, or was going to say;

He had difficulty with empathy;

He didn't know how to build or keep relationships; and

He was self centered and absorbed, and put his interests first.

Yes, on the surface, Neal appeared crude, impatient, indifferent, uncaring, and judgmental. None of these personal characteristics endeared him to others. People politely tolerated him or worked with Neal, because they needed to treat him as their "boss" or valuable "client." His children feared him and deep inside disrespected him. His wife, Nancy, did her best to keep his impatience, frustration, and anger to a minimum, but rarely stood up for herself or found her voice. She became an enabler, where fear was a primary motive for fulfilling Neal's needs. She didn't want him to take out his frustrations and anger on her or their children, and did her best to keep Neal on a tranquil path at home by subjugating her own needs.

In a sense, Neal was the bully at both work and home. He commanded people do as he wished. Otherwise, they would be at his mercy from tantrums of anger or shunned and the target of his dismay and dissatisfaction.

When Neal began to open up about his own fears and anxieties, he finally allowed his vulnerable side to emerge. It was a rather interesting dynamic, sitting across the table from this amazing powerhouse, and have him reveal, "I don't know quite how to say all this, but I think it is important you know I was raised in a household where my father was domineering and my mother was, well, just too passive. I was horribly afraid of my father as I was growing up—he was stern, a strict disciplinarian, and expected me to be a high achiever in academics and athletics. All I ever really wanted was an occasional compliment, or, if the truth be told, to have him hold or hug me—you know, just be tender with me. Instead, all I ever heard were messages directed toward how I could have done better, if only I had... whatever was relevant to the moment."

Neal had been tortured for years that he was not good enough: he felt that his successes only resulted when he was relentless and put work before family. No amount of financial success or the growth of his company assured Neal that he had arrived; that he was truly financially and professionally successful. He repeated the same pattern taught by his father... that achievements and the end results were what mattered, not the people in his life. Like his father, Neal also married a woman very much like his mother: patient, soft spoken, hesitant to stand up for herself, and friendly, with the ability to make small talk with other corporate and client wives.

Finally Nancy's resentment could not be stifled. She was no longer satisfied to be the good corporate wife and mother. Going into her 50's and yearning to fulfill her needs, she was tired of living to simply please Neal and to raise her family. She desperately wanted to be loved, to have intimate moments with Neal, to have fun with him, to do activities as a family, and to be heard and understood. She was tired of Neal, cutting her off—too busy and too disinterested to take the time to listen and fully understand.

The first point of emphasis and agreement in working with this couple was that each was responsible for one's own thoughts, feelings and actions and the change needed to start with each of them. Most couples erroneously think and wish the partner would change, and then everything in their marriage would be all right. The reality is that when the change starts within an individual, the partner responds to that change.

Neal and Nancy agreed to be open to change. They were taught new ways to communicate their thoughts and feelings, using "I messages," which is a process to share emotions, the reasons behind them, as well as their innermost needs and wants. The couple learned to take turns talking and listening, successfully hearing and understanding the pain that the other felt. In doing so, their compassion and tenderness toward the other visibly increased. Not only did their words toward the other change, they began to look more directly at the other as they communicated and at times held the other's hand, or stroked the other's arm if one would become teary eyed.

My HEART™ method featured Neal examining his relationships within his family. It was a red-letter day when he excitedly said to me, "Wow! I just realized I don't want to perpetuate the legacy of coldness and reaching career and financial goals at all costs like my father. I truly love my wife and children and want to learn how to be more loving, attentive, tender, and emotionally supportive."

Neal further conveyed how he wanted to engage with them more in quality activities and time together when they could smile, laugh, and confide in each other. He also changed his lifelong belief that work success was the way to love his family. Previously, Neal's vision of love was to buy gifts or to give his family what they wanted such as vacations, travelling, paying for expensive lessons and endeavors, and providing them a beautiful place to live. He now began to value family over work, making an important shift in his previous struggle between work and family.

Neal stopped being the taskmaster for himself and those around him. He learned to be emotionally supportive and more compassionate with himself, his employees and his family while treating himself and others with respect. He stopped being the combative, "know it all." Instead, he learned to listen to others' ideas and allowed them more freedom to implement their plans, adding to further growth and success of his company.

Neal likes himself now. This newfound self-acceptance and love are making life easier as he rarely abuses himself or others. He is much more pleasant to be around and is closer, more loving, and enjoys the times with his wife and family. Neal's ability to listen and to ACT on Love™ for himself and others has changed his life around. He's now living the dream that true success begins at home!

Chapter 7

"My Picker's Broken!" Looking for Love in All the Wrong Places

Love yourself first and everything else falls into line.

~ Lucille Ball (1911 – 1989)
American actress, comedian, model, film studio
executive, and TV producer.

THESE WERE ACTUAL words uttered to me in my first meeting with a coaching client named Maude. Her primary purpose for seeking me out was because she had endured disappointing and unhealthy relationships, which caused her to doubt her ability to pick a quality man as a lover and partner. Maude had reached her tolerance of dysfunctional relationships in which she felt controlled, unloved, rarely prioritized, and often disrespected. The words rushed from her, in deep waves of pain as she shared, " I just desperately want to feel the love, passion and tenderness I see everyone else having in restaurants, at the mall, and around town."

"My picker's broken" is the exact phrase that so aptly describes so many clients I have worked with over the years who unwittingly chose the wrong type of romantic partner. Through repeated experiences of being unloved, cheated on, manipulated, and often made to feel inadequate, unattractive, guilty, dumb, and helpless, these partners settled for whoever would pay attention to them and "love" them. At the core, the commonality was low self-esteem, in which each believed deep inside that they were unworthy and unlovable; that this was all they could ever attract and keep.

It's interesting too, that most of these individuals, including Maude, actually picked people who were "emotionally and physically unavailable" to them. Once unleashed, Maude's pain continued to fill the empty spaces in the room as she shared, "I don't know why I'm such a loser! I keep picking men who don't know how to truly listen and hear my pain... my excitement, dreams, and hopes. Over and over again—I pick the ones who can't emotionally or physically support me at any level!"

Like Maude, the mates being selected tend to be self absorbed and interested in satisfying their own needs and interests, not in working together to fulfill each other's desires. Again, like many others, Maude thought she could change her man. How wrong! Most often, what you see is what you get.

Like many others before her, Maude wasn't treated as unique or special as a child. She was deprived of attention and physical affection, and longed for someone who would give her these treasured gifts of love. Maude couldn't hide the way she really felt about herself. At every opportunity, Maude would put herself down, calling herself "stupid," and imploring, "What's wrong with me?" Even her unconscious body language, as she spoke with me, gave away her lack of confidence and sense of worthiness. Tears filled her eyes as she asked, "Do you know that I will quickly look away if I see a man looking at me? I have gotten really good at acting as if I am distracted by something in my purse; I look at my phone or look away in some quirky contrived manner." It was obvious to me, with her hastily shared words that when someone did actually speak to her, she would respond in a soft, low tone making it difficult to hear her, which more than suggested the meekness and hesitancies lying within.

Compounding her problems of attracting healthy eligible males, Maude also didn't believe she could approach men directly or initiate conversations with them. Waiting to be approached left her a "victim of circumstances," devoid of the power to let a man know that she was interested in him. Imagine the number of men this beautiful woman missed out in engaging conversations and relationships if only she looked up, smiled and said, "Hello."

From my professional experience, I could see that deep inside, Maude was afraid to trust herself to start a relationship with a man. The men in her past would present themselves as someone quite different from the man she got to know at the beginning of the relationship before she found herself falling for them. She began to be aware of the many red flags that appeared even when dating. As I discussed experiences with her, she suddenly blurted out, "I just know that I seem to be the one who does the majority of listening and asking questions. The men I pick... all they want to do is talk about themselves and never care to find out about who I am, what I like, or even want to know about my feelings."

We were able to uncover that Maude was naturally attracted to financially successful men that were used to "getting their way." They were the ones in command, and people listened to them while they talked and used their power. One man that she dated began to distance himself when she declared boundaries of no sexual contact for several months until they mutually felt affection and commitment toward the other. In all cases, they didn't know how to be compassionate toward Maude, or understand how she thought and felt about different circumstances and experiences. Furthermore, they didn't know and didn't have the skills to show emotional support.

As we worked together, Maude began to understand she didn't need to continue the legacy of her childhood... to be invisible and undervalued. She was encouraged to feel more loving towards herself and acknowledge and value the gifts within her. She began to realize she could actually create her own experiences and heighten her levels of attractiveness and be seen as a warm person to the opposite sex, rather than just another pretty face that seemed bored, preoccupied, arrogant, or self centered.

One day, during a brief follow-up session, I was excited to hear of Maude's success, "Oh, my gosh! I'm actually beginning to challenge the beliefs I acquired when growing up in my family. Now I am creating new rules that empower me, and allow me to open up physically and verbally as I greet new men I am meeting!" As a Coach, vested in her success, I was thrilled to see her confidence blossom as she eagerly absorbed and tried out the secrets I passed on about how to initiate conversations. She learned ways to have meaningful, intimate two-way conversations and how to truly listen to another to build deeper relationships.

Ultimately, the one thing I really wanted for Maude happened and she couldn't wait to tell me, "You can't believe how much more aware and alert I am to the red flags men show me. I now see that they're totally unworthy of further attention from me!" Hooray, Maude was making great strides in boosting her self esteem, her confidence, and feeling lovable and worthy!

With my encouragement, Maude compiled a list of "deal breakers," in which she could objectively break off unsatisfying and incompatible relationships and became more and more excited to try out her new skills in being magnetic to men. She immediately saw and felt the difference that her newly found expression of openness, warmth, and her stronger communication skills made in introducing herself and being present with a man. She is no longer an invisible, disinterested wallflower. In Maude's own words, "I am now in a relationship with a man who cherishes me and is a supportive life partner. My dreams are being realized more

each day, all because you taught me how to love myself—and
to risk taking steps to welcome men into my life."

Chapter 8

Angry Outbursts Finding Your Own Voice

When your emotions are greater and more intense than your situation, they are the accumulated remnants of your past, waiting to be resolved.

~ Mamiko Odegard

AS SHE GREW up Danielle was dominated by older brothers who told her what to do and didn't want to hear about what she needed. Over time, Danielle felt unimportant and learned to deny her feelings. Her parents added to the feeling that what she experienced and what she wanted didn't matter.

Fast forward to a woman in her 40's who grew up denying her feelings and not letting them out until it was too late! Danielle came to see me because she was alienating others with her overly abrupt and angry outbursts. As a result of Danielle stuffing her emotions, she tended to over-react and her emotions became too intense for her and others around her. Others would distance themselves from Danielle when she became upset.

After several unfortunate reoccurrences, Danielle had enough! She was tired of others ignoring or minimizing her thoughts, emotions, needs, and wants. Desperate to be heard and accepted, Danielle realized she needed to learn the skills to talk with others in a calmer, more rational way. In order to accomplish this goal, Danielle had to start with the basics of being in touch with her feelings. She also learned the damage caused by her fear, hurt, and anger, when she was loud... blurting out accusations, blaming, and over generalizing that she later regretted. She felt helpless and out of control when emotions would overtake her.

Together, Danielle and I discovered the secret of why her emotions were so difficult to contain as she opened up during one of our sessions, saying, "Each time there was a confrontation or outburst, I never had the opportunity to work things through and the hurtful issue was never resolved. I guess all that did was cause me to feel more anger, and feel violated, misunderstood, and devalued. I think I am coming to understand that I've had a lifetime of pushing my emotions aside and being labeled as needy or too sensitive."

Danielle also learned that she was often not in touch with her feelings because she lived on "auto-pilot" and dismissed her needs and wants as being unimportant and left them unmet, unknowingly leaving her emotions exposed and vulnerable to even more anger and hurt. As she became aware of her thoughts and the feelings that triggered her emotional outbursts, she began to give herself permission to express them whenever she recognized her emotions. She practiced skills of how to express herself by learning to communicate what was going on internally rather than attacking or lashing out. She then communicated in a more constructive manner and let others know her thoughts and feelings in real time — rather than suppress them for a later explosion. Others responded more positively toward Danielle by being more present to better listen and understand what Danielle was experiencing.

I count the honor of working with Danielle as a success. She recently came in for a follow up session and told me, "After all this time, I am free. I now understand why it's so important to be honest about my feelings and to express them at the time I experience them. You will be proud of me! I have also given myself permission to not only talk about my emotions at the time they happen, but also to be my genuine, authentic self. This being authentic thing... it has been the key to how I can really be intimate with myself and others, and truly let everyone know what it's like to be in my mind and body!" Needless to say, both of us were beaming with joy as I hugged and congratulated Danielle on her monumental accomplishments.

Danielle is more at ease and no longer lives in fear of disrupting her relationships when she is being honest about her thoughts and feelings. She can be more tactfully in tune with others' emotions and needs as well as her own and can now more readily show respect, love, and understanding to herself and others. By finding her voice, Danielle is finding respect and the closeness from others that she so desires.

Chapter 9

The Perpetual Caretaker
What About Me?

Taking care of your needs first is your ultimate gift… to yourself and others.

~ Mamiko Odegard

MANY CLIENTS HAVE come to me with problems from doing too much for others, while their needs and wants go unnourished. Many have been entrenched in beliefs and actions that they must take care of others and forgo their own needs and happiness. Unfortunately, to continually put others needs before yours is a formula for sadness, hurt, resentment, and a life full of longing and regrets.

Let me introduce you to Karen. She was the oldest of four children and as the first born, she found herself babysitting her younger siblings. Even before they came along, she was the stabilizer in the family, the one her family leaned on to take care of their needs, including those of her parents. Her father and mother were both alcoholics and were confrontational when drunk. They argued about money and jealousy, and would accuse the other of flirting and paying too much attention to members of the opposite sex.

Because of her parent's alcohol abuse and financial strains, Karen became overly responsible at a young age. She became the perfect child... or should I say "the adult in the family." It became quickly evident the kind of childhood that had shaped Karen, as she cautiously revealed, "I remember as a little kid how I would try to calm my parents by gently tugging on their arms when they got into arguments. Their screaming and yelling scared me! I think I just didn't want to have any reason for them to have complaints about my behavior. I also remember that over time, they each trusted me and I became the confidant for my parents, where they vented to me rather than blame and rant to each other."

What Karen did not realize, was that over time she became the mother and the surrogate marriage partner. She conscientiously took care of the younger children and the

65

home while her parents slept or partied. Unknowingly, Karen began to keep herself and her family safe from physical and emotional harm by becoming a master caretaker. She continually gauged the emotional status of each family member to prevent angry flare-ups and to ensure that their emotional needs were being met.

She began to sacrifice herself more and more, and by focusing on others, Karen lost touch of her own feelings, thoughts, and needs. She rarely thought of herself and suffered in silence, content to provide love to her family and sacrifice her own desires. Karen's personality became one in which she was overly controlled and controlling. Digging deeper into Karen's behaviors, which were being formed into what would ultimately become destructive life patterns, I was pleased to hear Karen's response to one of my questions, "Mamiko, I guess I just steeled myself. I just wouldn't allow myself to ever cry or to feel despondent. That is probably what caused me to become more serious. I even had difficulty laughing and being spontaneous or carefree like other kids I knew. What you are helping me to see is that maybe my control of the behavior of others wasn't from me being bossy or controlling, but living into my "experience" in trying to stop and reduce their fear, anger, or pain."

Karen found her way to me, because she realized that she was caught in a trap of exhaustion, frustration, and sadness. As an adult, she found herself starting to feel resentment that family and friends could be carefree and live their lives the way they wanted, while she remained under the pressure to be the compassionate caretaker. She didn't know how to change this self-defeating cycle of caring for others, but not herself.

Through coaching, Karen unraveled how she got to this place and where she wanted to go... to be more fun loving, and to not feel guilty if she did things to please herself. Above all, she wanted to give herself the same quality love and tenderness that she so freely gave others. A big shift for Karen was necessary to change her self-sabotaging belief that others' needs came first. She ultimately learned that prioritizing herself was actually self-care and love, because she could then give others a healthier gift of love, happiness, and being authentic of who she really was and what she wanted for herself and from others.

Sometime after our sessions had come to a close, she called me to share her progress. "I just wanted to call and let you know you really made a difference. Life is now a nice balance of meeting my needs first. I have become more loving towards my family and friends, and I feel a whole lot less frustration and anger... or feeling like a victim. I think you remember when we first met, I had this silly notion that it was ok to want—or expect—others to fulfill my needs and wants just as I did for them. Well, we both know how that worked! Unfortunately, the harder I tried to make others happy, the more exhausted, resentful of being used, and depressed I felt. Once you showed me how to give up being the rescuer I can now enjoy my life and the family and friends around me. Every day it gets easer to take that one step at a time, and share my needs, ask for assistance and understanding, and, oh... love the person I am rather than simply exist in a life where 'Karen' did for others!"

I was overjoyed to hear Karen now established healthy boundaries of when she chose to step in and help. Most of all, it was clear she was able to discern whether she was coming from a place of love and kindness or from a place of fear...

fear that someone would be angry, sad, create a scene, drink too much, etc.

There are countless numbers of you whose stories would mirror that of Karen. Some of you might be taking care of your children and/or your elderly parents. Are you struggling to do it all alone, being the one to suffer silently, only to vent anger towards the people you love? Or like the enlightened Karen, are you able to ask for help and be genuine about your true needs and feelings? Yes, you can show your greatest love to yourself and others when you ACT on Love™ towards yourself and show love freely and consciously to those near and dear to you.

Chapter 10

Addiction
The Devil Made Me Do It!

*Taking responsibility for your own behavior
gives you true power.*

~ Mamiko Odegard

HAVE YOU EVER obsessed over something and felt compelled to complete an action over and over again? Rationally you know that it's wrong and could lead to trouble, but your emotions over-ride your intellect. This is the definition of an addicted person whose downfall could be anything from gambling to sex.

Such was the case of Craig, a high-powered corporate executive who had risen quickly to the top. He came into my office, desperate to stop his drinking. It was jeopardizing his career, his marriage, and his family. Bored, stressed, and having little personal interaction, as he worked from home, Craig found himself hiding bottles of vodka and drinking throughout the day.

As with many alcoholics, Craig started drinking to ease the stress of demanding meetings as he flew across various territories to meet with his staff and clients. He would have to put on such a superb performance each time that he was exhausted physically, emotionally, and mentally by the time he climbed late into bed or hurriedly caught a flight back home. Craig's problem was further compounded by many late night meetings with clients, which included a full round of food, from appetizers to deserts, and of course, before-and-after-dinner cocktails. Due to the time demands of his work as well as managing different time zones, it became a habit for Craig to start having a nightcap in the privacy of his hotel room or home to relax. The drink on the plane was easy to access and complimentary to first class flyers and Craig enjoyed feeling important and having drinks on the plane as he justified his "reward" for a job well done.

Due to the temptations bred in isolation, by the time Craig sought me out, he was regularly drinking during the day. He sheepishly revealed his spiraling habits, "I'm okay having my first cup of coffee at 6 AM and looking at my schedule for the day, but by 10:00 AM, I find myself already sneaking my first drink as a way to ease into the day and prepare for the tensions I know I'll be facing. Around noon, I'll fix lunch and have another Coke and vodka. I'm ashamed to say that sometimes I drink so much that I'm actually drunk when I conduct staff meetings – during those times, for the life of me, I can't remember what I told them. I feel like a total moron and am so scared that I'll be tripped up... that others know I'm not right. I can't let it go that I'll slip up at meetings and won't remember what I promised a client or even what I had delegated to which staff member." As his fears and shame consumed him, Craig drank even more to "relax."

Addictive behavior is sometimes difficult to categorize as self-sabotage; there are so many elements that come into play, but when I first started working with Craig, I was confident self-sabotage was the devil in the dealings, as he poured out his heart in my office, "I just feel so burned out and lethargic! Although I recognize some of this involves the pangs of my guilt, this lack of energy puts me in a state where I rarely play with my young daughter and now, I am terrified as I become more distant with my wife. My life has become nothing more than a cycle of work and drink; devoid of energy or ambition to engage with my family. You have to help me!"

Further questions revealed Craig's underlying reasons behind his drinking wasn't to simply relieve anxiety. He recounted going to a highly acclaimed private high school and college, and how he had felt ashamed of his family's economic status and his father's occupation when he compared his to the lifestyles and prestigious careers of his friends' parents. He felt self conscious and out of step with his peers as he viewed them as more gifted, smarter, wealthier, and being exposed to more opportunities in school and in the professional world. In college, he started drinking alcohol regularly to have fun, be more relaxed, and to take on the leader and happy-go-lucky persona as he socialized with his peers. Inside Craig continued to feel inadequate and the more he drank to quench an uncomfortable stigma.

Through our discussions about the real reasons behind abusing alcohol, Craig came to understand he had risen to a high executive level, which he didn't believe he really deserved or could handle success. Although Craig was very intelligent, he was caught in a vicious cycle where he sabotaged himself with his low esteem. Because Craig wasn't confident he could handle a high level position, he unconsciously made poor decisions, which resulted in mediocre work results and difficulty with key staff members at work. The cycle of pressure from his uneven work performance had Craig abusing alcohol, eroding his confidence even more while escalating his fear of failure and getting caught.

Elevating Craig's confidence and esteem were critical to his sobriety and his self-imposed pressures. He realized his feelings of inadequacy were unfounded. He became acutely aware of when he would compare himself to others and rapidly stopped this habit. He was intelligent and competent, learning to live in the moment and self soothe. In a moment of revelation, Craig confessed, "I've been blaming other people and situations for my drinking. Now I'm seeing that it wasn't about them, but about me, disbelieving that I was worthy and had the skills to be at the top." Each session, Craig made strides in awareness of thoughts and situations, which caused him to be anxious and pressured while learning to emotionally embrace himself and quiet his doubts.

During these sessions, Craig was also taught a variety of ways to relax, to accept and nurture himself, and participate in AA. His success in abstaining from alcohol boosted his self-respect and his confidence about work. For Craig, the ability to forgive himself for his past was important for him to let go and to start fresh. Forgiving and loving himself, Craig turned his family life around, made them a priority and spent more time with them, and more carefully chose his travels, and safeguarded the temptations to drink in the hotel or on the plane.

The end of letting the devil have his way in Craig's life was a journey, but the amazing results shined through and Craig was ultimately able to proudly proclaim, "I am truly able to be my authentic self, freed of the emotional prison of putting up facades of being an important person. I can now come prepared and confident I have good solutions. To you… Mamiko, I am grateful for the many paths you showed me, so I could finally find myself and be the worthy individual I was destined to be."

Chapter 11

Social Anxiety
"Please Don't Pick Up the Phone!"

—————

When I let go of what I am, I become what I might be.

~ Lao Tsu (571 BC – 531 BC)
Philosopher and poet of ancient China.

DOLLY WANTED TO start a successful business, but knew she had to overcome her crippling anxiety and reluctance to meet or call people. She dreaded having to make a cold call or walk into a networking meeting. Even with people she knew, Dolly would convince herself that she would feel awkward talking with them. She was a bundle of nerves if she had to walk into a networking event and then would often stand by herself by the door, and wait for someone else to come talk to her. She had even convinced herself "people would be disappointed if they were somehow 'stuck' with her and had to talk with her when networking. "I don't have enough to offer people trying to make valuable connections. I'm a nobody!"

As Dolly shared the self-defeating thoughts, which prevented her from being relaxed, carefree, and being her true self around others, a common theme revealed she was extremely critical and judgmental of herself and felt others perceived her in the same light as they watched or talked to her. I could feel Dolly's angst as she commented, "God! Sometimes I feel so self-conscious, even if I am doing nothing more than walking across a room. I dread going to an event, even with people that I know, that I've actually turned my car around and gone back home instead. You are going to think I am totally weird, but even though I really want to be successful in my own business, I secretly hope whenever I call a prospective client, the person on the other end of the phone won't answer."

As I talked with Dolly, it became abundantly clear that she had suffered several traumatic events as a young child. However, the irony was that her natural child and personality was one of a tomboy and a daredevil. She thrived on taking physical chances where she could get hurt or be able to handle encounters with dangerous animals that others, even adults would be afraid of. She was highly independent as a young child and could take care of herself as well as being content to be alone and entertain herself for hours.

Dolly was the middle child and grew up in a home that lacked physical and verbal affection. Her father would take her to do activities with him or take her to get treats. Dolly was less attached to her mother. She didn't confide in her family and retreated most of the time to her room or playing outside. Dolly revealed that her mother had a miscarriage when Dolly was five years old. Her mother began to withdraw even more from Dolly... In fact, her mother experienced great anxiety and depression after the miscarriage, and became afraid to leave the house or to be in large spaces.

During our VIP one-day retreat, Dolly was able to understand that she had taken on her mother's fears. The fears of what others thought of her and being afraid of new situations were not Dolly's fears; they were her mother's. Dolly lit up, getting the big aha that she no longer had to carry these fears. The other big insight was that Dolly was actually letting her 5 or 6-year-old child make decisions and control her life! Dolly's child controlled her, not her adult self. Dolly was excited, happy, and relieved that she finally was able to piece together the puzzles of her life, which had long kept her down. Now she was liberated to be the easy-going, fun loving, and take risks person that she had been as her "natural" child.

Even when we had uncovered so much of the cause of Dolly's behavior and pain, her biggest question to me remained, "Mamiko, deep inside, I still wonder if I can ever be successful in making cold calls. Will you be able to help me connect with others and give me the confidence I can actually be credible enough to close the deal?"

After working on ways to overcome old destructive thoughts and beliefs, we put the call to the test. Dolly passed with flying colors! She was masterful at quickly engaging and drawing the other person to her while building trust and gaining a commitment to follow-up. Dolly was so personable, persuasive, at ease in her conversation that the prospect felt understood, respected, and eager to work with her. On the phone, words seamlessly flowed out of Dolly's mouth. I was completely in awe of Dolly and so proud of how warm, helpful, enthusiastic, and genuine she was in expressing her desire to help and provide hope for her potential client. She was every bit the confident professional that she wanted to be. She was truly a transformed person in less than eight hours of time.

During our meeting, Dolly's gratitude overflowed. I was touched by her personal growth and her sincerity; "My goal today was wanting to fully understand why I carried fear and feelings of unworthiness for so many years. You helped me find that! Not only that, I never dreamed that I would be able to let them go and claim my gifts of acceptance and love for myself. I wasn't so sure about all that child/adult conversation, but I wanted you to know "Dolly's adult is now in charge of my life and career!"

Chapter 12

Affairs of the Heart
It Takes Two to Tango

I have found the paradox, that if you love until it hurts, there can be no more hurt, only love.

~ Mother Teresa (1910 – 1997)
Roman Catholic religious sister and missionary.

KRISTIN AND ROLF contacted me just days after Kristin discovered her husband's affair. They were both distraught and confused with an overload of emotions. Rolf didn't know why he had started the affair; he knew only that he cared for another woman. Kristin wasn't able to get real answers that she was seeking and felt extreme violation of their marriage and trust.

After talking with the couple, they agreed to a 48 Hour Love Makeover™ to determine whether they could get past the affair. They were nervous and anxious whether this intensive retreat would work to repair the damage that had been caused and whether they could love each other again.

After over 30 years of marriage, various problems surfaced:

> Medical problems began to complicate their physical intimacy in which sex had essentially disappeared from their relationship;

> Kristin had stopped initiating sex, and Rolf found Kristin less physically attractive;

> Neither felt loved or cherished—rather they found themselves taking the other for granted;

> Neither knew how to truly communicate and be emotionally supportive of the other;

> Both found themselves being more critical of the other with expectations of how the other partner should behave; and

> Both were caught in everyday routines that yielded less fun and enjoyment with each other.

Rolf's desire for a sexual connection led him to search the Internet for "massages," which then spurred him to pay for sex. For several months, he maintained sporadic contact and began to have feelings for the woman with whom he had connected online, wondering if he were falling in love with her. As is often the case with infidelity, the lover who strays outside of the marriage beyond the relationship boundaries, often sees this secretive other person as exciting, attentive, and understanding. Thus, when the unfaithful partner returns to his mate, the relationship can seem even more disconnected, boring, and unhappy. It's interesting to note, too, that when a person considers leaving the marriage or committed relationship, it's tantalizing to think that the "grass is greener" on the other side and begin to focus on dissatisfactory behaviors that justify leaving the relationship.

Aside from hurting his wife, Rolf also worried about hurting the other woman. He cared about her feelings in breaking off the relationship, which caused even more pain and mistrust within Kristin.

Obviously there was a lot to discuss, which each did during their VIP retreat. The first thing that was addressed was each person's commitment to the marriage. After both fully agreed they were willing to give their best effort to determine if they indeed loved each other and wanted to save their marriage, they were introduced to ways to constructively communicate with each other so they could understand the feelings and reasons behind the other's actions. They each fully discussed their feelings and the questions they needed to have answered in ways that conveyed understanding of the other. Kristin discovered that Rolf had secretly been feeling turned off by her appearance and lack of self-care. She also learned how important sexual and emotional connection was for Rolf.

Rolf learned about how he had kept feelings deep inside all his life; he was able to finally reveal them. Rolf also began to hear and understand Kristin's deeper need to be loved and to feel cherished by him. Although each thought they were showing each other love, their actions were not being received in the ways the other wanted.

One fundamental aspect of working with any individual or couple is to guide them to stop blaming the other. Thus, an important turning point for Kristin and Rolf was not only to understand the other and be able to put oneself in the partner's place, but also each took personal responsibility for the affair happening. The couple could now see the tangibles as their relationship immediately regained closeness. Finally... they were able to be themselves and fully disclose their fears, needs, and hopes for the future.

In one of the sessions, the interplay between the couple was fascinating as they shared their feelings. Rolf took the lead, saying, "I absolutely know I made a bad choice in going outside of the marriage and hurting Kristin. I take full responsibility for not being honest about my feelings and needs to her."

Kristin, graciously offered, "I also acknowledge I had begun to take Rolf's love and commitment for granted. Over time, I just stopped doing the little things that made me attractive. I guess I wasn't very successful in 'reading his mind' to understand what Rolf really wanted from me."

Given the loving mindset and promise that each would do everything in their power to be honest and be open to keeping their marriage alive, along with a guided conversational style, they both began to understand the various ways to show love and the importance of letting the other know their innermost feelings and desires without the other having to guess or make assumptions of what the other wanted.

Rolf strongly committed to be faithful and to break off the relationship with the other woman. Choosing to let go of the past, each asked for forgiveness, and forgave each other, which was paramount to the couple reviving their relationship and feeling calmer, more trusting, and loving. They began to restore their trust in each other, and fully recommitted to their marriage and their love for each other by the end of day two.

Erroneous to common thought, an affair doesn't have to signal the end of a relationship. An affair can jumpstart a marriage by providing a wake up call that something is wrong within it. Even after several years, this couple continues to enjoy a revitalized marriage with each showing signs of love in multiple ways throughout the day. They both feel accepted for one's true self, understood, and emotionally and physically supported. This allows each to be even more closely connected and share their feelings as these arise. On a recent follow-up, Kristen gushed, "We're so much in love. We're using the tools you gave us and we're having the time of our lives. We can't thank you enough for helping us save our marriage." They appreciate each other even more, and realize how precious life is. Smiling broadly, Kristen voiced, "We didn't know we could be so happy again and be so much in love!" Rolf enthusiastically smiled and nodded in agreement. My heart melted with love and gratitude for the privilege and honor in being able to work with couples such as these two dear people and change their lives for the better—all because they dared to fully examine themselves and the intrinsic value of their relationship.

Chapter 13

The Loveless Marriage Do I Leave or Stay?

When two hearts come together to create more love, magic happens.

~ Mamiko Odegard

A COUPLE WITH whom I recently worked, came to me because they showed no passion in their loveless marriage. There was little physical affection or conversation. Months would pass without any sexual intimacy.

Melissa and Dan met in college and neither had much dating experience. They shared a class and worked on projects and assignments together, becoming closer friends. Dan took on the aggressor role and initiated the conversations. As Dan recalled the early days, he shared, "Initially, I was attracted to Melissa's face and body, and admired her intelligence and persistence. I liked that she was independent, goal oriented, hard working, and ambitious. I was really drawn to her, and thought that although Melissa was quiet, she possessed a can-do attitude and I admired how she would dig into her assignments, and produce top grades."

Dan believed that it was normal and customary to take the lead as talker and conversationalist. He also held big dreams of being successful and liked the idea of having a career woman as his wife. Over time, they became closer, even though Dan continued to take the lead affectionately the majority of the time. He was the one who wanted more loving gestures and was the more demonstrative of the two. Over time, Dan stopped initiating and began to be more critical of Melissa. Dan was also angry about Melissa's inability to prioritize him and their lack of regular sexual intimacy. Melissa, on the other hand, began to be more consumed with work at her investment firm. She would wake up early in the morning, study the early market indicators and head to work. She typically worked long hours in her demanding job to meet her quota. When Melissa was at home, she was frequently too tired to talk with or engage with Dan.

Melissa, too, shared her moments, "Well, I was first attracted to Dan's intelligence and his gentle manners. I remember always feeling so safe with Dan, knowing he would never be jealous or have angry outbursts that could result in physical and emotional abuse. I always felt it was perfect and natural that we fell in love and married!"

Their marriage had become like roommates, with each passing the other, sometimes without even a shared greeting. Dan obviously wanted more from Melissa, "I guess I really just needed her to give me a little undivided attention, and be more demonstrative, romantic, and interested in my activities."

Melissa was quick to speak out, "I found myself all wrapped up in being efficient and was fulfilled in being career-focused. I thought Dan knew how much I admired and loved him. He's an adult! I thought he'd understand that I needed to respond to the pressure to perform at the highest level with financial responsibility to my clients. I knew my success was something Dan and I would share."

"In the end, Dan said, Melissa's gestures to please me, such as going out to movies and dinner together and the occasional obligatory sexual interludes, left me feeling unsatisfied."

Melissa, on the other hand, noted, "I believed I was making genuine attempts to save our relationship. I know I carried hurt and resentment that Dan could be self-absorbed in fulfilling his career but not afford me the same consideration. In the earlier years, I even had to be like many women, juggling the demands of work and home, and taking on the primary parental responsibilities."

Now similar to other empty nesters, Melissa and Dan found that they shared few interests in common. They had little to talk about and when they did talk, it was unfulfilling with little listening, understanding, or emotional connection.

Neither had grown up in homes where there were outward demonstrations of physical affection and verbal encouragements. Each thought they were showing love in the ways that the other partner desired. Instead, they were missing the mark—neither really understood or knew how to show love. Love is not just about sex and physical touch; it also encompasses thoughtful gestures, having fun together, compliments and statements of gratitude, and sharing one's deepest feelings and desires in ways to promote really knowing the other.

Many couples make the mistake that when they go to a counselor or a coach that every conversation has to be serious about emotionally laden topics. I wanted this couple to fall in love again with each other and that was not going to happen with conversation. They were encouraged to simply enjoy each other's company and to find new and old interests to have fun together and to discover each other just like when they were dating. Only when they shared companionship and friendship while laughing and smiling and showed genuine interest in finding out about the other's struggles, hopes, and dreams, were they able to rev up their connection and affection. They prioritized their time together and choose activities to try, sometimes alternating between events that stimulated each of them. This couple's dates revived the spark and they began to enjoy the other's company once again. They realized the ways they had changed as well as the values that had initially attracted them to the other.

In the process of communicating true thoughts, intentions, and feelings, they were able to let go and resolve the issues from the past. As we wrapped up the balance of the program, each partner had something to say. Melissa started the conversation, "I understand more clearly the impact I can make when I take the first steps in showing affection. Although initiating affection was foreign in my family, I already notice a change in both of us when I take loving action."

Dan expanded, "Yes, we're each becoming more conscious of what we want, and sharing and showing what we want with each other. We are now coming to agreements about how to handle future situations so we can feel more understood, cared for, and loved. We have each asked for forgiveness for the harsh ways we have treated the other. Most importantly, I think, is that we have also learned how to forgive ourselves. Thanks to your guidance, Mamiko, this marriage was saved and reinvigorated... with love, empathy, and fun!"

Chapter 14

Prosperity or Poverty Mindset, Which One are You?

"The choices and the actions you take today create the future you desire."

~ Mamiko Odegard

IMAGINE... FLYING IN private jets and presiding over million dollar deals, feeling like a celebrity. Now imagine yourself hitting rock bottom. I recently worked with Joe, a man who had many financial and business successes in the past, only to be at the bottom financially, emotionally and lacking a base of new and regular business clients as well as missing a sustained loving relationship. When we met, Joe confessed, "I've lost my confidence and am getting in my own way!" There was an air of desperation and fear in his voice as he wondered how he was going to pay his rent and business expenses. He was down to his last few dollars in his checking account.

Joe found himself struggling with how to get going and attract clients, but kept getting distracted and demoralized by asking himself frightening questions about how his future would turn out. He was stuck in looking too far into a future for which he had no answers. Early on in our conversation, Joe expressed his feelings, "I seem to churn more anxiety in my brain, stomach, and body, and all it does is deplete my energy to be productive or motivated when I keep asking myself, "What if?"

This line of questioning evoked overwhelming and agonizingly different scenarios that could happen in the future. One of Joe's "what if's" led him down a quagmire of other unanswered questions, fueling even more doubts and feelings of being stuck. The first step for Joe was to rein in his apprehension of the future, stop these circular questions, and instead focus on what he could do now to have greater power to free himself from anxiety and create the income he so urgently needed. Joe immediately understood the fruitlessness to allow his mind to rule his emotions and actions when he tried to crystal ball the future.

This cycle of self-defeat continued as Joe mentally beat himself up for getting distracted and wasting time on nonproductive behaviors. "I'm robbing myself with time wasters and looming over stuff that I can't do anything about at this moment." One example Joe revealed was spending too much time obsessing over not having enough money to pay bills and degrading himself for being in such a dire financial bind. He would think about switching funds from one account to another. Instead of viewing the ways of transferring funds from different accounts as a time waster, I complimented Joe for being productive in finding workable solutions.

He was excited to finally be able to look at his actions in a favorable light, sparking his energy to be productive. "Mamiko! Thanks to you, gone are the days of aimlessly daydreaming in my car or at my desk. With your techniques, guess what—instead of all those crazy what if's, I can now spend my time strategizing the best ways I can financially prosper."

In working with Joe, he was able to see that he was his own worst enemy in not knowing how to emotionally support himself. That is why he felt so strongly that he had to have a loving partner that he could come home to who could encourage him. He began to realize that he needed to befriend himself first rather than looking at solutions outside of himself to be rescued by another person. As we talked about Conscious Loving™ Joe said, "I am really becoming acutely aware of just how badly I have judged and criticized myself. I'm finally learning the skills to change my perceptions of who I am." This was a major breakthrough for Joe as he also recognized how he immediately lost his physical, emotional, and mental energy whenever he disparaged himself.

Joe began to understand that even though he berated himself mentally, others picked up on his lack of confidence and lowered energy levels. Like so many of you, Joe had put up a smiling face as the exterior, to show everything was going well for him. Inside he felt like a fraud, pretending to be happy and successful. The internal conflict tore away at him and Joe wanted to reclaim the feeling he had the many years he built and sold multimillion-dollar businesses. He just couldn't get over the hump, and wanted help.

After just a few hours together, Joe was energized, enlightened, and excited about his power to change and the concept to "re-boot" himself. He enthusiastically declared, "At any moment in any place or time, I can completely realign myself!"

He was learning to incorporate the secrets to honor and love himself while staying in the moment, and the "aha" of changing what he could. "My, Gosh! I'm robbing myself by wasting time and looming on stuff I can't do anything about at this moment." By focusing on the past and the future, both over, which he had, no control, Joe had felt hopeless and beaten. Now, by paying attention to what he told himself in the present and taking action to make his life and situation better, Joe actually brightened before my eyes, feeling reinvigorated and hopeful. Imagine my joy when he said, "Positive events are already changing and happening for me!"

Like so many, Joe realized that he was exactly where he needed to be to dramatically turn his life around. Shame and failures from his past prevented him from connecting with his clients and a significant love partner. Each contributed to his reclusiveness and choosing to stay home rather than putting himself in situations where he would meet potential clients or women.

Discovering the origins of his shame as a young boy with his overweight appearance, and finding the importance he attached to how others perceived him, led Joe to relive his shame about failing in business and struggling financially. It wasn't long before Joe told me, "I have gained new insight into how the feelings of shame, which contributed to all my feelings of being inferior, actually helped me to overachieve in athletics and in school. That's how I became a leader way back then." He finally understood his inner need to succeed in order to accept himself, actually held him to intensely high standards.

Joe learned various ways to "reset" his energy, thoughts, feelings, and actions. He now felt that he had choices to benefit his motivation, productivity, and positive outcomes as well as to stop the comparisons to his more successful peers and release his shame. "Where I am right now doesn't define me!" Joe adamantly declared, affirming his worth and ability to overcome. He felt strongly he was now on the road to success, rather than sabotaging himself with nagging self-doubts, second guessing himself, or judging and punishing himself for his dejected moods and behaviors.

Prior to working together, Joe was also down on himself for the choices he made in pursuing women who were physically or emotionally unavailable. He habitually picked women who loved his success, the material benefits, and the physical love and attention he gave them. Unfortunately, these women didn't know how to support Joe emotionally or physically when life became difficult for him.

Joe committed to being his best self and was dedicated to healing himself first for at least two months before he would consider attempting to attract another woman into his life. Joe knew that by being his emotional and intellectual best, he would be attractive and destined once again to be the leader in business and successful in finding true unending love. Joe could also now be authentic and be accepted and loved for the person that he is. Grateful, Joe remarked, "I'm blessed even when I have failures and difficulties."

Yes, a total mindset change took place for Joe in just one day of our working together, and set in motion many rewarding outcomes. Through facing his difficulties, Joe was able to discover his higher self and ways to accept and love himself, and live a life enriched with much appreciation and gratitude. Now able to focus on and grasp opportunities for dramatic change in real time, he recognized and released blame for the past and actively stopped worrying about the future. I had reason to smile when Joe remarked, "I have transformed from victim to victor with a mindset of worthy abundance!"

Chapter 15

Emotional Eating
Filling the Emptiness Inside

*When you hunger for love, all the food in
the world cannot fill the emptiness inside.*

~ Mamiko Odegard

DO YOU FIND yourself eating, knowing deep down inside that you're not really hungry? Yet, you're unable to stop yourself, searching for comfort to fill the holes of loneliness, sadness, boredom, frustration, anger, anxiety, stress, and overwhelm? Whatever life throws at you, your best and most reliable friend has become food.

Nellie, a woman in her 50's, was a confluence of all these emotions. Upon meeting, she blurted out "I hate myself! I have absolutely no will power. I just hide in my home and eat. That's the only thing I know how to do when I feel so tangled up in my emotions. I'm hopeless... I'm out of control and trapped!" She was desperate to receive help.

Nellie's weight has ballooned up to 210 pounds, gaining over 65 pounds in five years. She had endured a number of life changes, starting with a painful divorce three years ago after her two children had left home. She recounted, "The last four years have been hell! I started going through the change of life over five years ago, having hot flashes, not enjoying sex, and being short and irritable with my kids and husband. Any little thing seemed to get to me. I felt repulsive and I could tell my husband was getting turned off by me more and more each day. He stopped making overtures for sex long ago... in truth I didn't really want sex, because it hurt to have intercourse and my desires had dropped way down. But I was really hurt that he stopped showing me affection and stopped trying to initiate sex. I wanted to feel like I still mattered and was sexy."

Feeling disgusted, ugly, and rejected, Nellie was emotionally compelled to unconsciously eat, primarily as a way to comfort herself. It started out with junk food and sweets. "I'd drive through fast food restaurants and order

103

hamburger, fries, and my supersized diet Coke and wolf down my meal in my car, hiding in secret. I prayed that no one would see me. I would feel so horribly ashamed that I would sometimes shake while I ate. I felt like a criminal who was going to get caught at any moment. To show what a loser I am, I would stop at another fast food or donut shop to have sweets or a shake, even just an hour or two later."

During the day, Nellie, a quiet homemaker, would feel restless and lost, as her children had gone away to college. Since her husband travelled for work, there was no regular routine of dinner on the table, activities, or homework. Her eyes filled with tears as she described those evenings, "Especially those nights, when left alone, I struggled even more with eating; craving chocolates, ice cream and anything salty, crunchy, and loaded with fat and calories." During those difficult times, she'd sit alone in front of the television, mindlessly eating and watching whatever programs caught her eye. It was not at all uncommon for her to eat almost a half-gallon of ice cream right out of the carton. On auto-pilot she ate without knowing if she were hungry or not. Over the years, Nellie had lost track of her real levels of hunger. As we later discovered during our sessions, Nellie realized she was too busy medicating herself with food to notice the signals her body gave her of being hungry or full.

Nellie's story is not uncommon, but in the heartfelt story she told, the depth of her despair became clear, "My life became an endless series of meals and snacking that never satisfied me. Each day, I felt more despondent, hopeless, and out of control. Not only did I feel bad about myself, I took on feeling of fear as my weight increased, so did my medical problems of hypertension, cholesterol, pre-diabetes, and various aches and pain. My body struggled on a daily basis to carry almost double the weight that I had in my 40's.

She was a heart attack waiting to happen and was on the verge of needing medications for diabetes. Due to her joint problems, Nellie had also abandoned any form of regular exercise. I saw both surprise and comfort in Nellie's eyes as I hugged her and reassured her that we were in this together. A little sparkle of tears welled up in her eyes as I shared how sincere my desire was to help her to feel beautiful inside and out, to raise her esteem, her love, and control over her weight. She burst into tears, feeling hopeful and grateful for my understanding and support. I clarified to Nellie that the path to her goals did not consist of quick weight loss ideas. Instead, she would be introduced to ideas that supported life changes.

As often reflected in my work with clients, I listened and affirmed the pain inside, quickly providing education of how Nellie was creating her own self-sabotage. Nellie immediately began to see just why she felt victimized by her weight and her eating habits, hijacked by her emotions, and the loss of love and divorce from her husband. She compounded the problems by frequently thinking to herself, *I'm so fat and disgusting, nobody would want to love me. I'm an ugly monster; they're staring at me like I'm a freak! I'm stuck— my life is miserable and I'm never going to change.* These thoughts pervaded the essence of Nellie and undermined her esteem, attractiveness, desirability, and hope.

After Nellie became aware of the unrelenting ways in which she took every opportunity to put herself down and reinforce how trapped she felt she was. Instead, she learned to instantly change self-defeating statements into those that provided her emotional support and nurturing. She didn't have to think in black and white terms of negative or positive statements; instead she discovered she just had to decipher whether she were criticizing and punishing herself or being affirming and supportive. When I asked her how the changes in thinking were working for her, Nellie proclaimed, "I can't believe it; I already feel different and lighter!"

Because Nellie was eating out of emotional distress rather than physical hunger, she was shown the HALT method, an emotional and physical "body scan" that she could use throughout the day and night. Whenever Nellie felt the urge to eat, I asked her to rate her hunger from 0 to 10 with 10 being famished. If she were truly hungry, then she was encouraged to "listen" to her body and to eat, but to choose foods that were more nutritious and in more appropriate quantities. Ultimately, Nellie was able to embrace the reality that often her food cravings had little to do with hunger. She was trying to replenish the "emotional hunger" of needing attention, love, and messages that supported that she was indeed worthy.

H stands for hunger: Am I hungry?

A represents anxiety and anger: Am I anxious or angry?

L equals loneliness and depression (sadness often accompanies loneliness): Am I lonely or depressed?

T means tired: Am I tired?

Nellie, began to utilize the four simple steps to determine if her hunger was emotionally based or caused by something else like fatigue. If the source of her craving was being tired, she was encouraged to rest or to take a short nap to refuel her body.

When emotions were the cause for her food urgings, Nellie was taught to do her detective work—to immediately stop and decipher her emotions and the thoughts that contributed to them. Completing the exercises, Nellie learned to instantly redirect and neutralize her damaging thoughts by lovingly being tender to herself. She didn't need to be overly enthusiastic and tell herself phony, positive thoughts she knew her mind would reject. When anxiety and tension got in her way, Nellie could use various relaxation methods that were easily incorporated into her daily routines. By using HALT, Nellie could actually go to the source of her cravings, rather than simply medicating herself with food. "Wow, Mamiko, now this all seems so easy. I can hardly wait to try out my skills."

Nellie began to realize that no matter how much or what she ate, she could not fill the void within her, and that she could now take responsibility for making better choices and taking action that immediately improved her life, emotionally and physically. She remembered as a young child that she was supposed to eat everything on her plate. Furthermore, food was amply supplied and encouraged in her family as rewards, for celebrations, and candy and cookies were abundant when she was sick, injured, or had a disappointing day. Instead of talking and confiding about her feelings to gain solutions... she gained solace through food.

An important part of Nellie's transformation was for her create the best relationship with herself, so she could feel comfortable and accepting in her own body. She was also taught how to share her thoughts, feelings, and desires and various ways to emotionally and physically connect with others for deeper relationships and intimacy. Nellie gained a new appreciation not only for her body but the essence of the person that she was, allowing her to more easily initiate reaching out to others to build friendship and support.

Nellie's weight is rapidly dropping as she feels a new sense of aliveness and love for herself. She has started regular exercise, focusing on small goals and achieving these with great relish and pride. Nellie is now radiating her inner and outer beauty. "Mamiko, I never thought I could feel so uplifted and happy again. Thanks to you, you've given me a whole new beginning!" The possibilities are now unlimited for Nellie, as she is claiming her own MVP rather than waiting for her life to change and for others to rescue her. She is creating her own ideal life and attracting even more love.

Chapter 16

The Talented Athlete

*Your talent is God's gift to you. What you do
with it is your gift back to God.*

~ Leo Buscaglia   (1924 – 1998)
American Author

ATHLETES PLACED ON the big stage can shrivel in the spotlight; they suddenly become tense and make minor mistakes that translate into bigger ones. When you know the win for your team is on the line, the stakes rise even higher, and your body instinctively tightens... unless you can master your mind. There is help and hope! Quieting your thoughts and maintaining your concentration is a skill, practiced over and over. Tiger Woods had it once; he dominated in such a fashion that his fellow golfers feared their fate when paired with him in the final round.

I would like to share with you the story of Bo, a young man who played professional football as a wide receiver. He could catch a football with one hand, sometimes making spectacular plays... as though he had Velcro on his gloves. To those who watched him, Bo appeared nearly flawless on the practice field—running smoothly, sometimes quickly cutting and then making a catch over his shoulder as though he had eyes in the back of his head. Yes, Bo was immensely talented; however, there was one problem. When game time arrived, Bo seemed to press too hard, and made both mental and physical errors. Catches eluded him, sometimes he stumbled, and was but a remnant of the practice player on the field... all of which puzzled the coach and his teammates with his erratic performance. Soon Bo was relegated to the bench, watching the starters.

Feeling confused and defeated, the situation prompted Bo to contact me. He wanted to work on his mental game, and regain the ability to be confident and dominate his game the way he had in practice. His uneven performance was easily noticeable to the team. No one could quite understand how this could happen to such a gifted athlete who—outside the game—could run, leap, and execute beautiful moves as he stretched and lunged for the ball. "I get so mad at myself; I can run and make those catches so easily in practice. What's wrong with me? I need to get this straightened out or I'm not going to last long in this league." His pain filled the room... yet my heart knew I could provide help and hope to transcend his problem to achieve consistent excellence.

The truth of the matter was that Bo was comfortable on the field and could almost flawlessly run and catch in rhythm during practice, because he was able to focus on the present. Unfortunately, when the reality of the actual game set in, Bo experienced intense anxiety each time he lined up and waited for the ball to be thrown his direction, Bo's heart would be racing as quickly as his mind. Instead of being able to concentrate on the moment, the young player's mind would shift his focus to past mistakes and worries about potential future errors. That replaying of the past and future mistakes and the resulting pressure to succeed caused his energy to immediately spiral downward making him slower and short of the target or having the ball squirt from his hands.

Similarly, Bo would also obsess, relentlessly running this pressure producing dialogue through his mind: *I've got to make this catch! I'm so stupid—everybody must be so pissed! Coach is gonna yank me. I just know it!* He was so busy playing the video in his head that he would forget where he was to be on the field and his timing would be off. Coaches did indeed quickly yank him from the game, knowing that Bo would most likely make more mistakes. The trust within Bo and his team had broken down.

A vicious cycle emerged. The more Bo was pulled from the field for making mistakes, the more the player focused on his errors, and unmercifully berated himself. Understandably, the cycle exacerbated the very mistakes he hoped not to make and took a hefty toll on his self-confidence. Bo was so fearful of making mistakes, that he soon became his own worst enemy.

When Bo came to work with me, we traced the history of his self-defeating performances. He realized he had never experienced anything close to the debilitating thoughts playing over and over in his mind when he was in public school or college. He also recognized that his playing ability had become markedly prone to errors when over-ridden with fears of failing. Bo came to understand that he was undersized and therefore, believed other players would be faster, jump higher, and would tackle him harder. Increasingly, Bo feared he would become another football casualty, and he shared those fears, saying, "There are other players who are a lot bigger and stronger! I seem to be plagued by the thought of dropping the ball, or being sandwiched between two guys who will swat or intercept it." Bo was especially fearful that he would "cough" it up when opponents brought him to the ground, knocking the ball from his cradled arm.

In Bo's mind, on the practice field, guys weren't trying to tackle him full force. In the real game, however, Bo was actually terrified of becoming a victim of knee injury, or other bodily harm that could dramatically end his playing career. Another discovery surfaced in our conversations. "In high school and college, I had been hit hard, but now, playing with pros who are so much bigger and stronger, I fear they are out to—or at least able to—disable me!" He was so fearful of being hit hard, losing the ball, and suffering a severe injury that he was continually distracted during the game. Bo became like the basketball player anticipating a foul; rather than focusing on the ball... for a nano second taking the concentration off the ball, contorting the body for the hit, and missing the basket. His repetitive thoughts of getting hurt and not making an important catch were displacing the automatic responses he had relied on as a stellar performer for so many years. Even on the sidelines, Bo would uncontrollably cringe and over-react to the sound and sight of clashing helmets and bodies slammed to the ground.

The hope and the help to redirect Bo were easy. We were able to increase his awareness of the immense impact his self-defeating critical thoughts had on his alertness, energy, and action. He quickly learned how to immediately recognize these destructive thoughts as soon as they emerged. Bo could then stop... and re-direct his thoughts to ones that allowed him to focus back on his playmaking. The new mantra that ran controllably through his mind was, *I'm staying in focus. I've run this route a thousand times before... just do what I naturally do. I'm fast; the ball is coming to me. They designed this play for me! The ball is landing securely in my hands.*

We were both excited when we saw how Bo had learned to coach himself and shift from the undisciplined fear, and talk to himself in a supportive way. He could now be honest and allow himself to vent and to fully express his fears of not being able to make it in this demanding league or being physically injured. Importantly, he was honing in on concrete strategies to end and change his previous anxiety and doubt laden messages.

To address Bo's fear of injury, he learned to imagine that by being smaller, he was actually faster and could easily slip away from the grasp of the larger lumbering opponents he previously feared. He practiced this mental rehearsal in his mind, smiled and anchored his confidence and renewed joy of playing football. Bo was also encouraged and taught to stay relaxed on the sidelines by staying in the moment and tensing and easing muscles to center himself and maintain a healthier balance of calm and energy. In our coaching sessions, Bo discovered the right keys for him to maintain optimal performance included movement, combined with focusing on each present moment in the game. Positive affirmations were also added to revitalize Bo's energy and mental focus.

A key to Bo's ultimate performance on and off the field was learning to forgive and to encourage himself. Forgiving and loving himself were the secret ingredients to up his game even more. Feeling at ease and peaceful inside his mind and body, Bo no longer needed to punish himself and relive mistakes after a game. Instead, Bo excelled in games just as he had in practice. Bo happily returned as a starter, feeling even more confident, powerful, sleeker, and faster! Yes, the gifted athlete had reclaimed his mojo and was having fun with his game.

Chapter 17

Loving Yourself to Success
Five Strategies for Creating
Your Best Life

*You can search throughout the entire
universe for someone who is more deserving
of your love and affection than you are
yourself, and that person is not to be found
anywhere.
You yourself, as much as anybody in the
entire universe, deserve your love and
affection.*

~ Buddha

I HOPE YOU have been inspired by the journey to greatness by the extremely brave and dedicated individuals and couples described in the previous chapters. They were each like you, sharing their fears, vulnerabilities, and doubts about whether they could achieve their goals. Yet, they all took a chance, feeling tired of the old patterns that enveloped them and left them feeling trapped. They, like you, dreamed of a life that was easier and one that produced joy, freedom, and ease, and regularly sought the positive adrenaline rush that occurs when you truly are in love with yourself and your life.

The steps toward you being EXTRAordinary make overcoming self-sabotage doable and achievable. Tap into the following secrets of loving yourself and creating your ultimate life:

Start with awareness: Not knowing where you are going and lacking a blueprint or plan to get there opens the door to self-defeat. Unless you are aware of what you want to achieve, you lack direction, motivation, and consistency. Common to all the cases presented, these individuals and couples all knew generally where they wanted to go. They were, however, without the knowledge or skills to navigate themselves to the life they so yearned.

The truth is all change begins with awareness. To help you to create your own awareness for life and work success, complete the following ACTivities. You may also find it helpful to organize all your thoughts, emotions, actions, and progress in a journal or on your computer. Alternatively, you can head over to my website and request a PDF copy of the accompanying workbook, which will make it easier to complete your answers directly under each question, and refer to it from time to time as you make progress on your transformational journey. You can make that request here: http://bit.ly/OSSActivityGuideRequest

Five Strategies for Creating Your Best Life

I. DEFINE YOUR GOALS AND OBJECTIVES

In order to succeed, you must first know where you want to go.

Are you looking for more business success?

What is your business success going to look like, feel like, and sound like?

Do you measure monetary increase as your achievement with an appropriate time line?

Most importantly, how are you bringing yourself closer to your goal?

Do you want an overall goal such as having more love in your life? If so, how is this measured and manifested?

Does this mean that you learn how to initiate and start conversations with strangers, participate in new activities, physically and verbally show affection such as increasing hugs, kisses, compliments and recognition, read self-help books or hire a coach to build your confidence and esteem?

ACTivity 1: Setting Goals

List as specifically as you can what you want to achieve. If possible, make it measurable to let you know if you are getting closer or shifting further away from your goal.

> This example, is written in an ambiguous manner, and makes it difficult to measure whether you are moving closer to – or away from – the goals you intend.
>
> **My Goal #1 Example:** "To accept and love myself fully and unconditionally."
>
> This is a much more clearly defined example:
>
> **Example**: Increase self-acceptance and love by acknowledging/complimenting myself with at least three statements that honor myself, or my accomplishments, each day.

Now write your own:

Ways to achieve my goal: (**ACT**ion steps I'm taking to reach goal)

> Example (s):
>
> Actively recognize and compliment myself at least three times daily.
>
> Whenever, I am judging or being critical of myself, I change this to a supportive, affirming, loving, or neutral thought/statement.
>
> I write and read daily affirmations that I create about my uniqueness.
>
> Now write your own ways to reach your goal:

Goal #2:

Define another goal you want to achieve, and document ways and the steps necessary to achieve it: (**ACT**ion steps I'm taking to reach goal)

Goal #3:

Define another goal you want to achieve, and document ways and the steps necessary to achieve it: (**ACT**ion steps I'm taking to reach goal) Repeat these goal setting steps with any additional goals on which you choose to focus.

Unless you are aware of the ways you harm yourself and prevent yourself from fully loving yourself and enjoying maximum success, you will repeat the same sabotaging behaviors over and over. Successfully overcoming personal deficiencies with changes in thinking, feelings, and actions requires you to be alert and perceptive to fine-tune your observational skills so you can catch yourself and change course before you spiral down to your typical and often automatic non-productive habits.

In taking the first step to manifest your healthiest self, draw on the support of a person who understands your pitfalls, experienced struggles, has triumphed over pain and blocks similar to yours, and can see things and guide you toward the finish line. Otherwise, you only know what you currently know and tend to repeat self-defeating patterns. An enlightened teacher, mentor, or coach can facilitate your awareness and show you the shortcuts to hasten the fulfillment of your goals.

In business and life, you want to ask yourself on a moment-to-moment basis, "What's the fastest way to reach my goal?" Many times throughout your day, you have the opportunity to take yourself closer to your goal or further away from it. "Contaminating" your goal is one way that my own coach, James Malinchak likes to explain how we sabotage where we want to go. Either you're getting "closer" to your goal or moving further away by "contaminating." These are the two "C's" that James' emphasizes about success. Can you go through this process alone, or would you benefit from a partner who is vested in you to successfully navigate your way to acceptance, love, and peak performance in the quickest amount of time? All great athletes, business executives, homemakers, celebrities and even students have had people who consistently guide them to be their optimal self. You are no different! You deserve to have quality people in your life who can jumpstart and maintain keen levels of awareness with new information, insights, and skills. Believe it or not, this is one test of how much you can love yourself... by being generous to yourself and investing in your own financial and relationship capital, and the all important relationship with yourself.

ACTivity #2: Surveys and Inventories

Conduct an honest, soul-searching inventory of the ways you think and act that sabotage your goals and happiness and list your findings in your journal or the ACTivity Guide you downloaded from my website:

http://bit.ly/OSSActivityGuideRequest.

Fortunately, there are myriad ideas to promote healthy changes in your life and business. As an additional bonus for my readers I have created a checklist of qualities and actions for optimal performance in every area of your life. You can opt-in and receive a PDF download for your own personal inventory at my website:

http://bit.ly/OPSSOpPerformCKLST.

As you go through your own checklist, and become more aware of the ways you strive for happiness and your optimal life, you'll reinforce the areas in which you exercise healthy emotional and personal wellness, as well as areas that you may want to improve.

II. MAKE A COMMITMENT TO CHANGE

Are you ready in your heart and mind to say, "Yes!" to become the person you dreamed of with the lifestyle that you desire? If you can honestly and enthusiastically answer with a resounding "Yes," then you'll want to write down the reasons why you are committed to making changes to claim your best self. Writing solidifies the covenant you choose to establish with yourself to change.

Only you can change yourself. No one else has power over you. If you do not fully accept and love yourself, no one can convince you to do otherwise. The critic within you cannot be convinced of the inner flaws no matter how much you gain compliments, recognition, physical affection, or even sex! Worse yet, when you don't fully love yourself, your closest supporters—friends, family, or even your lover—give up, because instead of meeting and reciprocating their loving intentions, you withdraw, complain, or demand even more love and attention.

When you feel unworthy and whatever you do is not good enough, that is exactly the same message you give back to others... that their efforts don't satisfy you or are simply not good enough. Your loved ones, in turn, will respond to you with impatience, frustration, and anger and back away both emotionally and physically at the very times you crave and need even more tenderness and understanding.

Yes, you are central to the ways you feel and the effect you have on others. By changing yourself, you actually influence positive changes in the quality of your relationships. This is the concept of "give to get," rather than waiting for your partner, family, friend, or teammate to change, you give away what you desire. By doing so, you create a circle of goodwill, which starts the movement of others to treat you differently, reciprocating with more of what you've given. In other words, kindness begets kindness, and love makes the world go around.

ACTivity #3: Reasons to Change—"My Whys"

List the reasons that you want to change for the better to create your best self. The main thing is to go at least five layers deep to uncover the real motivation for you to change. When you identify that core need and desire, you will have a powerful ally to bolster you to success. Some of the following reasons or "whys" may exist for you:

I'm tired of being so critical.

I don't want to be depressed and anxious any longer.

I'm tired of struggling alone and want a soulmate who understands me and gives me support.

I have hope that I can change my life.

My ability to love myself will lead to loving others and getting love in return.

I have personal freedom to achieve and gain the love and happiness I'm seeking.

I let go of my fear of rejection; instead I feel empowered and secure to give myself love and approval.

Now grab your journal (or workbook) and list your own reasons for changing to a healthier YOU!

This exercise has been designed to help you develop a greater degree of self-awareness. In addition to the actual self-discovery, it is equally important to address how you feel after completing this **ACT**ivity. Take a few minutes and list some of your Aha's.

III. LEARN THE ART OF CONSCIOUS LOVING™

You walked into a trap of being critical and diminishing your self worth and love. Stepping out of that and into Conscious Loving allows you to think of yourself, others, and situations through new perspectives. You are able to withhold and change your previous critical and judgmental reactions with fresh ways of looking and interpreting actions and emotions to ones that are more tender, loving, and supportive. This allows you to start over and cherish your uniqueness rather than dwell on your deficiencies. Mindfully loving yourself in this manner doesn't imply that you have to be a rah-rah cheerleader, needing to interpret your feelings and behaviors in an overly positive light. Instead, it is learning to be gentle with yourself, and giving yourself the "benefit of doubt," so that you stop judging, berating, and putting yourself down.

Conscious loving is about freedom of choice. Each and every moment, you are faced with choices of how you want to perceive, feel, and respond to various situations. It involves a moment-to-moment awareness without judgment so you can make the best possible choice for the most favorable outcome. It also requires you to refrain from being critical of yourself or others and to strive for neutrality. If you are unable to affirm a supportive outlook, then aim to be neutral in your thoughts and impressions. Conscious loving is allowing the powerful and highly refined state-of-the-art camera of your mind to take multiple photos simultaneously, within milliseconds, of any and all events of your life. The skilled photographer takes numerous shots and carefully examines each one to determine the best image that he or she has captured. Similarly, you repeat the same process, choosing the picture that will most likely yield the best perception and results for you.

It's important to center yourself into a state of calmness to enable you to most effectively choose the picture or scene that will give you the best outcome. It is human nature when you are emotionally aroused that your thoughts mirror your emotions. For instance if you are angry or scared, your thoughts are consistent with these emotions, justifying your reactions and actions. Therefore, returning to a calm state is a necessary ingredient to foster best choices and outcomes by using both your mind and emotions to guide you.

To practice conscious loving, take time to re-examine any critical thoughts and patterns of judgments that cause you to lose energy, focus, feel discouraged, derailed, and feel less worthy. Imagine you are using a high-powered camera within your mind, and take on a perspective of acceptance to rewrite new beliefs and thoughts that promote your highest self. Are you noticing any changes in your body and the way you now feel towards yourself? When you affirm yourself, you instantly boost your energy, motivation, and feelings of worthiness.

A word of caution! Understand this is a journey, not a marathon. I want you to experience small steady steps to success to build your confidence and esteem. Conscious loving is a lifelong skill. You weren't born with it; you aren't supposed to automatically know how to put these steps into action. Mindfully loving yourself is a skill you develop and will come more naturally to you as you engage in new ways of viewing yourself and everyone around you. It gives you the power and means to embrace and stand by the greatness of yourself and others... allowing you to fully love without limits.

ACTivity #4: Developing Awareness

Brainstorm the typical ways you downgrade yourself and keep a notepad with you to write down thoughts when you find yourself being critical of yourself or others.

What are you telling yourself; what patterns to you notice?

How do you feel as you criticize yourself or another?

Do you believe these messages?

What are your payoffs for keeping these messages?

How do these critical thoughts/messages undermine you?

ACTivity #5: Assess Feelings

Only when you honestly seek to be open to new awareness and better understand yourself, will you find the answers hidden deep within. It is sometimes far easier to live on the mere surface of life, but when you take time to ask how you really feel about yourself, you can discover the rich treasures of transformation. You'll be surprised as to how new insights and changes in your thoughts can foster new feelings and actions. The following activities will assist you with that process.

Write down thoughts and feeling as they come to you.

Go back to ACTivity #3 and read your original reasons to change; if the work you have done thus far has had an impact, you may feel enlightened and want to modify your reasons for change. (This helps you to recommit to changes you deeply desire.)

ACTivity #6: Deeper Examination

Begin to examine the sabotaging beliefs that you carry that somehow you are unworthy, less than, not as smart, attractive as others...

Doing your own detective work, look back to your earlier years as a child and adolescent and examine your memories and beliefs from them.

How did you feel then?

What were your experiences?

How were you defined; who defined you?

Write down old beliefs you acquired?

Do you recognize any common themes?

What new insights emerged for you?

ACTivity #7: Promoting Positive

Create and write down new beliefs and rules about yourself that promote feelings of appreciation, gratitude, and love for the person that you are.

These new beliefs promote warmer, more secure, and confident feelings about yourself with guidelines to steer you toward healthier, more productive and loving choices and actions.

How do you feel in creating new operational rules and beliefs for success?

How do you feel about starting anew?

If there is any old baggage still remaining, reach out to a professional coach, mentors, loving family and friends.

Write down your action steps now.

Enjoy your sense of freedom and power! Smile and enjoy the feelings that go along as you take steps toward love and acceptance of self.

IV. LET GO OF PAST MISTAKES AND FORGIVE YOURSELF

If you continue to focus on choices and actions you regret, you drain both your energy and motivation, and also feel overwhelmed and defeated. The past is already gone; you cannot change it. Living in the past causes you to have regrets; bringing up waves of shame and guilt. It also robs you of enjoying and appreciating the gifts of living in the present.

ACTivity 8: Release and Start Anew

Once again, use this **ACT**ivity Guide and write down all the mistakes, regrets, and shortcomings you would like to release... to feel free to start anew. Using only the language you so aptly carry in your head, spew out the loathing and blame you commonly use to undermine your value, credibility, and yourself. It is likely you have elevated your feelings with some of the previous exercise, and you may feel an immediate shift with this ACTivity as you think of blaming yourself and convincing yourself that you are "stupid, worthless, ugly, don't have enough to offer another, not a good conversationalist," etc.

ACTivity 9: You Don't Have to Be Perfect!

When finished, review your critical branding and lists of mistakes and use the lists as further motivation to seek your highest version of yourself. You don't have to live with pain; you DON'T have to be PERFECT! Take time to write down any feelings and experiences that have become more positive as a result of the work you have completed in previous activities.

ACTivity 10: Love Letters

Now is the perfect time to write a tender loving letter to specifically forgive yourself. Please make sure you show compassion and understanding to the less enlightened, younger you who committed these errors. You can also use this time to include any shame you are holding.

You may want to close your eyes and listen to gentle, soothing music before you write your loving letter. You may also find it beneficial to do a peaceful meditation and visualization prior to forgiving yourself to get yourself in the "flow." Visualize yourself physically letting go of your past and forgiving yourself. Of course, you can repeat this process whenever desired, before, during, and after as you work toward forgiveness.

ACTivity 1l: Letting Go

The process of letting go is best if not left to passively thinking your way through. Put your emotions and energy to these statements and say them out loud! "I forgive myself fully and completely; I let go of any and all past mistakes. I let go of the past... I am starting over."

Follow your verbal proclamation with a ritual for letting go of your mistakes, blame, guilt, and shame. This could involve burning your list of your painful past, burying them, letting them sail away on a little toy boat, drawing a picture representing your pain, and replacing it with a picture that represents your present and future happiness and peace... whatever facilitates your letting go in a more actionable manner.

If necessary to truly free yourself, go back to the steps in ACTivity 10 to let go of any hurt or anger you hold toward another by writing a loving letter toward that person where unfinished feelings exist for you. You want to clarify how you have been angered, threatened, disappointed, betrayed or hurt by another.

When you forgive yourself, you tear down the barriers that prevent you from succeeding. You also learn how to accept and love yourself. You aren't perfect, nor are you meant to be. You are in the process of learning to cherish yourself so others can also treasure and support the wonders of you. In turn, you learn to accept others the way they are rather than taking such strong positions they must live up to your expectations of them.

V. ACT ON LOVE™

Your ACTion list is not fulfilled until you take time to embrace and celebrate the new improved version of yourself; knowing that you are starting with small steps, which can make dramatic differences in arriving at the destination you choose. It's important to start with tiny achievable goals that you easily reach and then progressively fine-tune and increase the level of difficulty, commitment, and effort. In each case, you want to ensure success in your milestones, not accept defeat.

Instead of becoming overwhelmed; think about the methods used to train animals, even as monstrous in size and ferociousness as a whale. First steps would include throwing fish out in the water so the animal approaches you. After repeated trials in which 100% success is ultimately achieved, you begin to toss the food closer and closer, continuing the process until the goal is achieved when a gigantic creature approaches you even when you hold no food in your hands

A concept known as *successive approximation* is what I want you to remember. Not many of you were taught the skills to truly succeed in life. It's unrealistic to think you could know how to magically change your thoughts and your energy to quickly and easily attain the goals you seek. Similarly, the majority of you were not taught how to truly love yourself or others, or how to handle disagreements. In fact, more often you witnessed the extremes: no conflicts or its opposite, raging and loss of control during arguments or bouts of anger. Is it really fair or rational for you to have an incomprehensible, impossible mission to always hold the perfect thought, quip, or response to perfectly handle all challenging and emotionally charged situations in your life?

Each time you reach any objective or goal, reward yourself with a smile, jumping for joy... where you instantly feel recharged and alive, congratulating yourself—in written form—or verbally in your head. Conscious actions to share your breakthroughs with a friend, family member, significant other, or supportive co-worker are encouraged... to help you claim your own magnificence and to debunk the erroneous myth that "you should not be boastful." Only you know the small and large battles you conquer. You no longer need to be the suffering victim or martyr. Instead, use your newly gained skills and mindfully choose to allow others to join in the celebration of a more impassioned, fun, spontaneous, and iridescent you—a you that glows with a love for yourself and your life. Allow your best-self and most-remarkable life to be continually upgraded to an "ultimate performance" that equates to the ways you show up in every aspect of your life.

The common element in all the stories of overcoming sabotage was learning to love yourself and others no matter what problems or blockages you face. Without loving and cherishing yourself through kind, considerate acts of self-care, you physically and emotionally erode. The biggest secret of all is that your power to believe, to change, and to claim your greatness was within you all along... hidden deep in your heart and mind. By bringing them to heightened levels of awareness, you can claim your best self and the rewards that accompany your journey. May you find much love, happiness, and success in all areas of your life! Celebrate your new beginning!

About the Author

DR. MAMIKO ODEGARD is the leading authority on love, relationships, and high performance; with over 30 years of  experience as a highly sought out professional life and executive coach, psychologist, individual and couples therapist, and seminar leader. She has helped thousands of individuals and couples to be and feel EXTRAordinary and to find happiness and success. Mamiko is known for getting dramatic life-changing results in hours, days, and weeks—rather than months or years! She has literally saved at-risk-marriages from divorce and helped couples to thrive and be closer than ever before, even after they've experienced an affair! With her bold coaching style, myriad women and men have overcome self-sabotage and settling for less than they deserve in partners, financial abundance, business success, and joyful lifestyles. She has also worked with people who want to excel in their fields such as musical artists and athletes.

Dr. Mamiko has been happily married to Greg, the love of her life, for more than 40 years. She and Dr. Greg were interviewed and honored as *The Couple of the Week* on the Dr.

Laura Berman Show, Oprah Productions. Because of their deep love, Mamiko was inspired to write about the ways to show love in an international best selling book, *Daily Affirmations for Love*. She is also the co-author of other award winning books such as *The Voyage to Your Vision* and *Miracles, Momentum, and Manifestation*. As the Emotional Wellness Expert, she writes monthly on relationships for Smartfem Magazine and for the Trivita Wellness Journal. Mamiko received Strathmore's 2012 Who's Who Worldwide Professional Award as the Life Coach of the Year, has served as the President of the El Paso Psychological Association, and currently is the co-chair of the Arizona Asian Pacific Women's Giving Circle. Philanthropic at heart, Mamiko also assists the founder of an international charitable foundation, The Perfect Day.

Providing content rich and skill building seminars and retreats, participants experience her wisdom in topics such as: Manthology: Getting More Love and Attention from Your Man; Loving Yourself—Loving the Caregiver; 365 Days of Love: Making Relationships Even Better; Abundance Beyond Money—How to Attract Your Ideal Relationship: Client, Business Partner, or Mate; Igniting Your Inner and Outer Beauty With Love and Style; Balancing Home and Work; and Reaching Your Goals—The True Secrets to Overcoming Self-Sabotage.

Greg and Mamiko have a daughter, Mariesa, who completes their circle of love and adds richness to their lives. Passionate about her work, Mamiko maintains a private coaching practice in Scottsdale, AZ.

She can be reached at:
Phone: 480-391-1184
Success@DrMamiko.com | http://www.drmamiko.com

Other Books by the Author

Delivering heart-felt messages has become second nature for Dr. Mamiko Odegard. You can access them on:

Her website: http://www.drmamiko.com/

Amazon Author Central:
http://bit.ly/MOdegardAmazonAuthorCentral

Barnes & Noble:

http://bit.ly/MOdegardBarnesandNoble

Daily Affirmations for Love: 365 Days of Love in Thought and Action
(Amazon International Best Seller)

Without quality relationships, you seriously limit what you can accomplish in life. *Daily Affirmations for Love* is 365 ways to learn how to experience the closeness, romance, passion, joys, peace, and dreams that are possible in all relationships. It can be used daily to recognize, remember, and celebrate the love and warmth toward a special someone in your life. The most important relationship is the one with yourself and you will find ways to strengthen the love within you, allowing you to more fully share and receive love.

Daily Affirmations for Love is not just about romance! To truly succeed in all areas of business and life, you must also develop and maintain life-long quality relationships with those with whom you do business, the people who know you intimately, and the family and close friends who support you with encouragement and affection. Through insights and activities, you also learn how to love yourself more deeply. Yes, the relationship with self as the core is the most important relationship of all. When you can truly love yourself, you can then more easily share love that enriches not only yourself, but all those around you.

It is the author's hope that this book will be shared with others. These expressions of love through verbal communication and acts of kindness can be shared with lovers, parents, children, and friends. Though practical steps, Dr. Odegard guides you to a new and heightened awareness, and provides tools to help you connect with others in life... with depth and love.

Miracles, Momentum and Manifestation: The Miracle of MAN-i-Festing the Ultimate Love Relationship (Amazon Best Seller)

Self help; dealing with couple and family issues, love and relationships. We are all confronted with them from time to time...

In *The Miracle of MAN-i-festing the Ultimate Love Relationship* Mamiko Odegard, PhD illuminates many fear-based beliefs and thoughts, each of which undermines healthy love and ultimately leads to suffering and tragedy in our relationships.

This chapter in *Miracles, Momentum and Manifestation* picks up where *Daily Affirmations for Love* left off... Mamiko Odegard builds on many of the principles found in her first best-selling book. Here she explores, at a deeper level how to shift from "wishing and hoping" to using a tried and true blueprint to "MAN-ifest" the kind of love, respect, and devotion you deeply crave. If you're ready to go for the gold, then read on, and build some momentum in your quest for an ultimate LOVE relationship.

Odegard helps readers discover certain truths she believes accelerate quality changes in relationships. Accessible and practical, Dr. Mamiko's wisdom invites you to look at your own life and see how MAN-i-festing a quality relationship can shift your relationship to one where you more quickly claim your true desires by cultivating a deeper awareness, detaching from unhealthy beliefs, and ultimately... discovering your true self.

Throughout *Miracles, Momentum and Manifestations* stellar writers contribute their journey to find each... with an underlying message of hope that defines when life happens or YOU can happen to life! In this anthology, eight authors share super successful Miracles and Manifestation concepts as dynamic and transformational experts—all leading to a better place in what we call an intentional LIFE!

The Voyage to Your Vision
Top Experts Chart the Course for Your Professional and
Personal Journey to Success
(Amazon International Best Seller)

We all have the capacity to become what we want to be, and achieve what we want to contribute to the world. Each of us is blessed with unique skills and abilities needed to become successful. On the path to success, we undergo a wonderful and adventurous voyage. In the recently released book, *The Voyage To Your Vision*, experts from across the globe gather to share the wisdom from their vast experiences with others and change lives during turbulent times.

Making the decision as to what we want our life to look like personally and professionally is not an easy task, as it requires the balance of our abilities, skills and passion. However, if we are clear in our choice, our minds and actions will be gracefully guided on the path to reach our goals. Being successful is not just about reaching the goal; it an also measured by what we are willing to do in order to see our mission fulfilled.

As we experience challenges, we become stronger, when we are willing to share these experiences with others, they can become invaluable, change lives and help others define and achieve their success.

The Gratitude Book Project: Celebrating 365 Days of Gratitude

The Gratitude Book Project: Celebrating 365 Days of Gratitude People from all walks of life join together in this

141

collection of essays-one for every day of the year-about the things, people, circumstances, and events they're grateful for. Need a pick-me up? How about a gratitude adjustment? Look inside-you'll be grateful you did.

Celebrating 365 Days of Gratitude is brimming over with appreciation and inside you will find evidence that harnessing the power of gratitude can be a life-changing force. These true life stories are about more than the polite "thank you" we casually exchange every day. They're testimonials to the people and things we often take for granted. Join us in this growing movement of people from around the world who have committed to asking themselves this simple yet profound question every day of the week-what am I grateful for? Net proceeds from the sale of this book go to support Feeding America, the American Society for the Prevention of Cruelty to Animals (ASPCA), and Women for Women International.

The Power of Letting Go: How to Heal Yourself & the World

In the *Power of Letting Go*, experts from all over the world share their stories and advice to help you let go, move on, and finally heal. It is no secret our world can be intense. Learning how to let go of pain or weight (emotionally and physically) for instance starts by learning how the pain manifested in the first place. Over a dozen experts across many professions share their advice and stories to help you embrace the power of letting go each day and begin to heal yourself.

*Explorer's Guide to the Law of Attraction
How to Tap into the Quantum-Heart for Happiness and
Success*

Explorer's Guide to the Law of Attraction: How to Tap into the Quantum-Heart for Happiness and Success explains how the Law of Attraction works, why it works, and how to make it work for you!

The book explains the philosophy behind the Law of Attraction and related principles; its underlying science of quantum physics, takes you on the author's spiritual journey of self-discovery, and gives you a road map for your own personal development

Reader Bonus

Note: You'll want to opt in below to receive your irresistible reader bonus items valued at over $500.

1. Complimentary *ACTivity Guide/Workbook*.
   http://bit.ly/OSSActivityGuideReq

2. Personal assessment, *Inventory for Optimal Life Performance in Relationships, Love, and Career.*
   http://bit.ly/OSSReaderBonus

3. Daily Affirmations for Love Sampler—First 30-days.
   http://bit.ly/OSSReaderBonus

Request for Reviews

Thank you in advance for taking the time to post a review for the book on Amazon; many readers will not take that step to purchase and read... until they know someone else has led the way.

If you enjoyed reading *Overcoming Sabotage* I would appreciate it if you would help others enjoy the book, too.

LEND IT. This book is lending enabled, so please feel free to share with a friend.

RECOMMEND IT. Please help other readers find the book by recommending it to readers' groups, discussion boards, Goodreads, etc.

REVIEW IT. Please tell others why you liked this book by reviewing it on the site where you purchased it, on your favorite book site, or your own blog.

http://bit.ly/OSSCustomerReview

EMAIL ME. I'd love to hear from you.

success@drmamiko.com

If you would like to be the first to read my upcoming books, subscribe via my Amazon Author Central account:

http://bit.ly/MOdegardAmazonAuthor

Made in the USA
San Bernardino, CA
01 April 2016